Spirit of the First People

D1127220

SPIRIT OF THE FIRST PEOPLE

Native American Music Traditions

of Washington State

Edited by Willie Smyth and Esmé Ryan

Introduction by Vi [taqʷšəblu] Hilbert

Published for Jack Straw Productions, Seattle

Northwest Folklife, Seattle

Washington State Arts Commission, Olympia

by the University of Washington Press, Seattle & London

This book is published with the assistance of a grant
from the National Endowment for the Arts.

Library of Congress Cataloging-in-Publication Data

Spirit of the first people : Native American music traditions of Washington State / edited by
Willie Smyth and Esmé Ryan; introduction by Vi (Taqʷšəblu) Hilbert.
p.   cm.
Includes bibliographical references and index.
ISBN 0-295-97732-9 (alk paper)
1. Indians of North America—Washington (State)—Music—History and criticism.
I. Smyth, Willie.   II. Ryan, Esmé.
ML3557.S7   1998
780'.89'970797—dc21   98-17704
CIP   MN

Contents

Foreword

THIS BOOK IS A COMMEMORATION—AND A LEGACY—OF A PROGRAM presented at the 1992 Northwest Folklife Festival. A collaboration between Northwest Folklife, the Washington State Arts Commission (WSAC), and Jack Straw Productions, the project was named "Spirit of the First People" by Skagit elder Vi [taqʷšəblu] Hilbert, a member of an advisory council which, over the course of two years, shepherded the event from concept to reality.

"Spirit of the First People" began in 1991, when we met with Willie Smyth, then newly appointed as WSAC's state folklorist, to discuss a collaboration that would expand Folklife's modest Native American program. After years of presenting the folklore of Washington's many cultures, it was clearly time to honor the First People by bringing statewide focus and attention to them, using a major visual arts component.

With support and cooperation from tribes throughout the state of Washington, we assembled an advisory council to explore and shape the possibilities for such a project. Bringing diverse backgrounds and viewpoints together, the council created an educational and exciting process for all of us, and it was an honor to be part of this remarkable group. Working on a daily basis with the council was a fascinating experience, filled with joy, surprise, and, naturally, many points of view. In the past, Northwest Native Americans had guarded their culture from the world's gaze; some felt this was still the best road to follow. Nevertheless, in the end our advisors said they felt "it was time"—to share their culture with the people of the state of Washington.

It is hard to convey the excitement we felt when the festival weekend finally was upon us. All over the grounds of Seattle Center, Native Americans in both traditional dress and street clothes were singing, dancing, telling stories, carving, or just hanging out, meeting new friends or renewing old acquaintances, or visiting with extended family from around the state. On the lawn by the Bagley Wright Theatre, the electricity in the air was palpable, as 500 spectators crowded around the two lines of seated players, facing off in the bone game. At the Flag Pavilion, after a moving ceremonial dance, one young girl from Wapato implored the audience, "Remember your past," and they leapt to their feet with approval and applause. At the symposium, Cliff Sijohn mesmerized listeners from behind a seminar table, with an amazing story about the power of song (see his essay) during a battle in the Vietnam War. At the exhibit, visitors wept in front of vintage black-and-white photographs of the old tribal schools, where Native Americans had once been punished for speaking their own language. As all of this unfolded, then folded back in on itself, a transformation occurred: For the first time, it seemed to us that the Folklife Festival really had accomplished our mission of cultural sharing and community at the level we had always envisioned.

"Spirit of the First People" has had a lasting effect. The trust and confidence built in 1992 has led to the development of a Native American music program and curriculum for elementary schools, an annual Native American concert at the festival (entirely curated and funded by local Native communities), and a compact disc of Native American songs from Washington State, included with this book. We are honored to be associated with such an important project of the Native American people of Washington State, and we are proud to share it with you.

Joan Rabinowitz	Scott Nagel	Willie Smyth
Jack Straw Productions	Northwest Folklife	WSAC

Preface

~

On what is now known as the Olympic Peninsula there lived an old man who was the last head whaler of the Coastal People. In his old age his wife gave birth to a son. This was their first child and the only one in the tribe who could inherit the father's whaling position.

As soon as the boy turned twelve, the old man wanted to take him to sea to teach him how to whale. People from the village protested, saying that the boy was too young; but the father, knowing that he was aging, felt he could wait no longer. One morning they gathered their crew and set out to sea.

When they spotted the first whale, the crew brought the canoe up to it, and the old man, poised beside his son in the bow, sent his harpoon into the whale's back. As the rope played out, the coils grabbed the boy's leg and pulled him into the water. A long time passed as they searched frantically for him. The stricken father was blaming himself for not listening to the village people, when suddenly the boy surfaced, barely breathing, but still alive.

Plucking him out of the water, the old man and his crew rushed back to the village. There the people expressed great anger at the old man's actions. For four days and nights the boy lay unconscious. Then he arose from his bed singing a *beautiful song. At the end of the song the boy told the people what happened when he was underwater:*

"The whale told me to crawl down the rope to him. As I did this, a bubble of air from his blow hole surrounded me. Then the whale began singing a beautiful song. I hung on and listened. When we started toward the surface, we came through different layers. Each layer was of a different color and had a different song. Each song was more beautiful than the last. Then, when we surfaced, I fell asleep."

The whale gave the boy not only his life, but also the gifts of song and color for his people. Before this time the world had neither music nor color. Guided by his experience, within four months the boy assembled his own crew and brought back the largest whale ever seen. He had become the head whaler of his tribe.

THIS TRADITIONAL QUILEUTE STORY CONVEYS THE IMPORTANCE of both song and oral tradition to Native people of the Pacific Northwest. It is a story about song giving life. Songs, like other kinds of art, have much power—the power to revitalize, to renew, and to create new life. They have the power to transform lives and to keep traditions and cultures from dying.

Many tribal cultural leaders in Washington feel that now is the time for songs to be sung. Like the aging father in the Quileute tale, many Native American tradition bearers fear the loss of valuable expressions of their culture. Both song and story have been a means through which knowledge and practices have been preserved and passed on. Like the aging father, some Native American cultural leaders are taking bold steps to protect and preserve traditions. They are seeking to renew these traditions with sacred power—power which revitalizes youth and keeps their culture strong and healthy.

Many of the state's leading educators and cultural leaders, both Native American and non-Native, hope that by educating Native American youth about the richness of their heritage, and teaching non-Natives about Native American culture, this empowerment of tradition will occur. To that end, a group of Native American cultural leaders entered into a project with the Washington State Arts Commission, Northwest Folklife, and Jack Straw Productions to share their song and dance traditions.

A collaboration with individual traditional artists and tribes from throughout the state began. The name "Spirit of the First People" was given to the project by

Vi [taqʷšəblu] Hilbert, one of the principal advisers. The keepers of song traditions and the cultural leaders on the advisory board assumed roles parallel to the elder in the whaling story. The three folklife organizations became comparable to the whaling crew.

It was agreed that a gathering of traditional singers, dancers, and elders would be an appropriate venue for honoring keepers of Native American song traditions and would be the foundation upon which the subsequent book and recording would be based. This took place at the 1992 Northwest Folklife Festival and was composed of an exhibit, performances, and a symposium where elders, Native American cultural leaders, and experts on Native American music gathered to discuss the most pressing issues in the process of preserving and perpetuating Native American music traditions.

The success of that unprecedented gathering of traditional singers inspired us to present the art and information shared there to a wider audience. The participants, who are now authors of articles in the book and singers of songs on the accompanying recording, have expressed their desire that all people have a deeper understanding of their culture. They have seen that the written word is a powerful tool for breaking down stereotypes and building bridges through human understanding and mutual appreciation. The participants in this project also see this documentation as a valuable opportunity to preserve selected aspects of their traditions for the future generations of their own tribes.

The format and content for this book and recording closely follow that of the symposium, exhibit, and afternoon of performances held at the Northwest Folklife Festival, May 22–25, 1992. Many of the book's chapters were prepared by participants in the symposium who also gave oral presentations of the same material at that event. Additional chapters were created to further document the exhibit and performances or to include additional perspectives. This book, however, is not meant to be a comprehensive account of all Native American singing traditions in Washington State.

The Native American advisers invested an enormous amount of trust in us and our ability to assist in presenting, in a culturally appropriate way, the knowledge conveyed throughout this project. What we had to offer was our experience in ways of honoring and presenting traditional cultures via such methods as public events, the production of educational materials, and our commitment to shared educational goals. They, on the other hand, tirelessly assisted us by navigating the project through the often difficult processes of decision-making.

We hope that this book will be valuable to Native American tribes in the state as a means of recognizing and honoring important tradition keepers, and of conserving traditional knowledge and activities. Our intention is for it to be equally meaningful to non-Native American readers who seek to better understand and appreciate the richness and significance of Native American traditional culture.

It is also our wish that this sampling of the rich traditions of our state will spawn future projects covering new territory that we could not reach, and that these rich traditions will long endure.

WILLIE SMYTH

Acknowledgments

SPIRIT OF THE FIRST PEOPLE: NATIVE AMERICAN MUSIC TRADI-*tions of Washington State* is a collaboration between Northwest Folklife, the Folk Arts Program of the Washington State Arts Commission, and Jack Straw Productions. To assure the accuracy, quality, and appropriateness of the exhibit, symposium, and performance selections, we called upon some of the most important Native cultural leaders in the state as advisers. These people offered consultation, contacts, and advice in a tireless and generous fashion on the Festival, the recordings, and this publication. For their kind help we wish to thank:

The Consulting Council

Colville Confederated Tribes: Adeline Fredin and Mary Marchand
Makah Cultural and Research Center: Maria Parker Pasqua and Helma Swan
Sacred Circle Gallery: Steve Charles
Skokomish Indian Tribe: Bruce-*subiyay* Miller
Tulalip Tribes: Sheryl Fryberg and Hank "Kwi TlumKadim" Gobin
Upper Skagit Indian Tribe: Vi [taqʷšəblu] Hilbert
Yakama Nation Cultural Heritage Center: Brycene A. Neaman
Quileute Indian Tribe: Lillian Pullen

We would like to thank the sponsors of Spirit of the First People: the Boeing Company, the Burlington Northern Foundation, the King County Arts Commission, the King County Cultural Development Fund, the National Endowment for the Arts, the Burke Museum of Natural History and Culture, the Washington State Arts Commission, and the Washington Commission for the Humanities.

For her hard work and vision curating the exhibit we would like to thank Roberta Haines. For the photographed artifacts in this publication we are grateful to the artists and lenders: Ernest Barr, Jr., Rodney and Colleen Cawsten, Greg Colfax, John C. Burch, Shelly Burch, Sonny "Nytom" Goodwin, Debbie Johns, Ron Lauzon, Bruce-*subiyay* Miller, Spencer McCarty, Bertha Visser, Colville Confederated Tribes, The Cheney Cowles Museum, The Legacy Ltd., Makah Cultural and Research Center, and the Snoqualmie Tribe. We also thank photographer Ray Fowler for endless hours of photographing artifacts and Lou Corbett for taking great photographs of performers in the midst of the chaos of the Festival. The exhibit could not have happened without the help, support, and lending of objects by Robin Wright and Rebecca Andrews of the Burke Museum, Seattle.

We would like to thank all of the performers for graciously sharing their songs for inclusion in the Spirit of the First People compact disk. For their tireless guidance in producing this CD, we thank Vi [taqʷšəblu] Hilbert, Linda J. Goodman, Brycene A. Neaman, Laurel Sercombe, and Loran Olsen. Special thanks to Father Thomas Connolly and Lawrence Johnson Productions for the recordings of the Spokane/Coeur d'Alene singers.

Performers from throughout the state were at the concert and were included on the recording. They include: Pauline Hillaire and the Setting Sun Dancers, the George Family, Fred Hill, Sr., Martin Louie, Bruce-*subiyay* Miller, Johnny Moses, Neil Moses, Lillian Pullen, Rising Son Drum Group, the Sijohn Family, the Selam Family, the Spokane/Coeur d'Alene singers, the Swan Family, Jeanette Timentwa, and Helma Swan.

We would like to thank the original symposium participants and the authors of the articles of this book, including Pamela Amoss, Virginia Beavert, Rebecca Chamberlain, James Everett Cunningham, Roberta Haines, Tillie George, Linda J. Goodman, Bruce-*subiyay* Miller, Brycene A. Neaman, Loran Olsen, Lillian Pullen, Laurel Sercombe, Cliff Sijohn, Jeanette Timentwa, Anne Renker, William Seaburg, and Helma Swan. For their hard work, we would also like to thank Susan Libonati-Barnes, Leila Charbonneau, and Annamary Fitzgerald. In addition, we are grateful to the staff of each participating organization for their dedication and collaborative effort.

The Project Staff

Jack Straw Productions

Joan Rabinowitz, Executive Producer; Tom Stiles, Doug Haire, Alan Leny, and Eric Bowerman, Recording and Production Engineers.

Northwest Folklife

Scott Nagel, Executive Director; Annie Jamison, Production Director; Paul de Barros, Program Director; Roberta Haines, Exhibit Curator; Nancy Worden, Exhibit Designer.

Washington State Arts Commission

John Firman, Executive Director (1988–93); Karen Gose, Executive Director (1994–97); Bill Palmer, Acting Executive Director (1997–); Willie Smyth, Folk Arts Program Coordinator.

Federally Recognized Tribes of Washington State.
Courtesy of Washington State Department of Ecology

Note: *The Samish Tribe (recognized in 1996) does not have a reservation. Samish Tribal offices are located in Anacortes in Skagit County. Final recognition is pending for the Snoqualmie Tribe and the Cowlitz Tribe. The historical area of the Snoqualmie Tribe is the general vicinity of the Snoqualmie Valley, largely in King County. The historical area of the Cowlitz Tribe includes Cowlitz County and parts of Lewis, Skamania, and Clark counties.*

Spirit of the First People

Vi [taqʷšəblu] *Hilbert.* Photograph by Jill Sabella;
courtesy of Washington State Arts Commission

Introduction

VI [TAQ^wŠƏBLU] HILBERT

WHAT COULD HAVE BEEN MORE APPROPRIATE FOR THE QUIN-
centennial year of 1992 than to have the Northwest Folklife Festival present an event
celebrating the spirit of the First People of Washington State? Five hundred years
after the arrival of Columbus, the First People still retain most of the traditions practiced by their ancestors. Performances and an exhibit of art and artifacts illustrating
these traditions were part of the event. The First People proudly responded to an invitation for each cultural group to present their ancestral treasures. Some of the songs
and dances normally done only in the privacy of an audience of the First People were
carefully selected for public presentation.

There was a quiet joy in the glances exchanged by all participants, expressing
the immense pride of groups sharing the most beautiful aspect of their culture: spirituality in song and dance. The general public was for the first time allowed to experience these riches, and this small sample of what has always been practiced created a
hunger to know more of such beauty. This book and the recording "Spirit of the First
People" may ease some of that hunger.

Traditionally, leading families from each area maintain and transmit the sacred
knowledge of their ancestors. Responsible members of each family inherit the right
to use this information when and where it is culturally appropriate, for there is a
proper time and place for each ritual. Outsiders are not allowed to participate, nor

would any of us disgrace the unwritten law that only family members of the group may perform or sing a sacred song or dance. This is an inherited privilege.

In my thirty-five years of talking to and with the public, I have found, at every age and educational level, a lack of awareness of the very presence of the First People and a lack of understanding of our culture. There is a constant need, it seems, to present some basic information for those who wish to call Washington State their home. We, the First People, share our land with you newcomers, and we expect you to learn how to apply the teachings of our ancestors in honoring and nurturing all things that we share. *A Time of Gathering*, the beautiful publication that accompanied the Washington State Centennial Exhibit (1989) at the Burke Museum, goes a long way toward helping to educate the reading public.

Because we carry on our culture through oral traditions, we can best help others learn by allowing them to listen to those things that can be shared verbally. At the "Spirit of the First People" performances at the Northwest Folklife Festival, many listeners thronged to hear our talented storytellers, who traditionally were, and still are, our teachers. Through stories, our ancestors taught us our commandments, philosophy, history, geography, genealogy, and drama. Learning an oral tradition taught us concentration, and helped us listen well in order to be able to retell what we had learned. There was no written language. We had to remember everything that was important, and that certainly excluded the superfluous and superficial.

The members of each cultural area in our state practice their traditions in the special ways passed down by their ancestors. None of them do the same thing in the same way. There are different languages for each group or tribe.

The music of our people represents, again, their individuality. Among the Lushootseed people, each person may earn or inherit a song that is his or hers to use for as long as life exists. Although the practice of questing in order to earn the right to such a song is now mainly a part of history, many of our people do indeed earn the right to inherit the strength of ancestral songs. The initiation into our longhouses, to become members of our ancient spiritual practice, is a very demanding discipline for the initiate, but it also includes the entire family.

Our Lushootseed longhouses, or smokehouses, are not open to the general public. The spiritual practice is sacred and protected from the casual onlooker. Although some groups allow outsiders to witness their spiritual practices, they identify and maintain ownership of certain inherited rights, which are respected by all other tribes or groups. When we hear the songs or the music from each area, we immediately recognize and respond with pleasure and delight to this privilege. We honor the practices of all people, and we rejoice that these teachings are maintained.

The things that have now been written were told by respected historians whose responsibility was to safeguard them until they could be transferred to coming generations through the written word. (Much of what was told by our Lushootseed historians has now been written.)

You, the public, are acutely moved by the strength of our spirituality. You feel, and can respond to this, as you listen to and watch our representatives, young and old. This is real, this is true. This is a living part of the past. No official, government, or church can negate the ancestral teachings. We are born with the genes that are a part of nature's instincts. Our Creator gave us the knowledge to access the spirituality of our earth.

The sacred will ever be sacred. What is the definition of sacred? Very simply and profoundly it is this: That which can be destroyed but not created.

The things we have had remembered for us down through the centuries are those that have borne the test of time and have survived because they were, and are, very important to the future of our culture.

VI [TAQᵂŠƏBLU] HILBERT is an elder of the Upper Skagit tribe. Since 1967 she has worked to preserve the language, literature, and culture of the Lushootseed people; she is the director of Lushootseed Research, a nonprofit organization dedicated to this preservation by sponsoring oral history collections and related projects. Her publications include the updated *Lushootseed Dictionary* by Dawn Bates, Thom Hess, and Vi Hilbert, published by the University of Washington Press in 1994, and three books by Lushootseed Press: *Aunt Susie*, by Vi [taqʷšəblu] Hilbert and Jay Miller (1995), *Gram Shelton*, by Vi [taqʷšəblu] Hilbert and Jay Miller (1996), and *Lady Louse Original Stories*, edited by Janet Yoder (1996).

Singers, Dancers, Dreamers, Travelers

Native American Song Traditions, Musical Instruments,

and Dance Regalia in Washington State

ROBERTA HAINES

THE EXHIBITION "SINGERS, DANCERS, DREAMERS, TRAVELERS" offered a glimpse of the musical traditions of the First People in Washington State. Dance regalia and musical instruments were the heart of the exhibition. The exhibit was originally conceived to showcase regalia, but our research found an entire world of sound that gave life and meaning to the garments and instruments. The exhibit's soul took shape from this elemental form of communication as the transformative power of ubiquitous song traveled with us.

The exhibit, then, became a vehicle for the songs that are the legacy of Native people in Washington State. These songs cross every kind of barrier: physical, political, social, and spiritual. They mark individuality and link the strong with the weak, the new with the old, the familiar with the strange. Our new task was to seek the manifestations of song in regalia and instruments that went beyond the limits of official ceremony to personal ritual, community healing, ordinary work and extraordinary play. This article documenting the exhibit is arranged the way the exhibit was designed, around the themes of living musical tradition and experience of the indigenous people in Washington State, but it will require the willing participation of your own imagination to hear the song in the rustling materials and tinkling ornaments and to feel the drum as you ponder the descriptions.

An important theme of the exhibit was to recognize the strength of indigenous traditions in the face of evolving historical events and challenges. The entry artwork (Plate 1) captured the city of Seattle's rich indigenous spirit that remains amidst the towering structures of modernity.

Despite the many obstacles that Native communities faced, the spiritual embers have never been extinguished. Often, as the exhibit showed, Native peoples gather in ceremony and celebration, changing from street clothes to skin gowns or cedar robes and capes to take part in the rejuvenation that is accomplished through dance and song. Singing provides the fabric for social communication, physical transformation, and spiritual expression.

Throughout the state there are shared music traditions: ceremonies at the beginning of various harvests; gambling; and winter gatherings for spirit dancing. Songs are part of the healing arts and child rearing, the center of social exchange, and a part of major life events, including births, weddings, and funerals. While winter ceremonies take a variety of forms, their essence is spiritual communion and development through song.

On the Olympic Peninsula, music is treated as a valued property right with a place in the political and economic hierarchy. Dramatic performance and inherited music and dance dominate most community activities. Composers of songs are valued artisans and paid for their inspirations. The Puget Sound peoples have a less formalized system than on the Olympic Peninsula, yet through marriages, family, and political alliances, the care of song is a valued property. Music in eastern Washington reflects a much different cultural perception. Anyone might create a song spontaneously. Some songs do belong to a particular people, some are inherited through spiritual transmission, personal dreams, or visions.

Persistent Traditions and the Ban on Tribal Gathering

During the nineteenth century, the United States attempted to "civilize" and "Americanize" the indigenous people by banning traditional Native practices. The Office of Indian Affairs remained under the Department of War until 1849, when it was transferred to the Department of the Interior. Its agents treated many reservation people like prisoners of war. Traditional practices and public gatherings, including dancing, gambling, and spiritual activities, were not allowed. Some agents restricted people from leaving the reservation, and most business that involved land or resources was federally supervised.

Fourth of July Celebration, 1903, Colville Confederated Tribes, Nespelem, Washington.
Courtesy of Cheney Cowles Museum, Berk Collection

Chief Skolaskin, San Poil prophet, Colville Confederated Tribes.
*Photograph by William Brain Coll; courtesy of Washington State University Libraries,
Historical Photograph Collections, neg. 92-054*

Tulalip Treaty Day Celebration, Tulalip, Washington, January 22, 1915.
Photograph by J. A. Juleen; courtesy of Tulalip Tribal Archives

Strong resistance came from many directions, including the isolationist and independent San Poils in eastern Washington. Chief Skolaskin was a controversial leader who challenged the authority of the United States and protested government intervention in his territory, especially refuting the Dawes Allotment Act of 1887. He was imprisoned without a hearing on Alcatraz Island in 1889 and not released until 1892, after the San Francisco press and national Indian rights organizations exposed the injustice.

Military-like control followed Native people throughout the state. Reservation "Indians" were required to carry an identification card, called a "Blue Card," that stated their status. Although U.S. citizenship was legislated in 1924, some states withheld voting rights to Native Americans until the civil rights movement of the 1960s.

Denied political rights and First Amendment rights of U.S. citizens, including the rights of free speech, free association, and freedom of religion, Native people in Washington State met the challenge to their national identities and cultures in creative organizing. While some traditions went underground, others were reorganized around practices acceptable to the U.S. officials. For instance, when citizens of the United States celebrated their own "independence," Native people also could gather and celebrate without offense. Throughout eastern Washington there have been gatherings, since the turn of the century, called "Fourth of July Celebrations." And tribes who had treaties with the United States found that they could safely gather around the commemoration of their treaty date. Thus "Parties" for public events in western Washington and "Treaty Day Celebrations" were born.

Spiritual Traditions

Despite persecution, the spiritual beliefs and the traditions of the First People continued to find expression. Like other traditional aspects of Native life, some of the spiritual traditions went underground while others incorporated elements of impinging Christian beliefs and practices. From about 1870 to 1900, a great evangelical Protestant movement swept the United States. Since their own religious freedoms were being denied, members of the Native community were drawn to the movement through "organized" faiths that developed inspired blends of Christianity and traditional Native spirituality. Acceptable to the outside world in form, Shaker churches housed the indefinable spiritual practices of the First People and provided a safe way for them to share their beliefs with each other.

Nevertheless, traditional spiritual leaders throughout the state continued to practice their beliefs with renewed vigor. In a surge of Native revitalization beginning in the 1850s, Smohalla, a Wanapum prophet from the Plateau, expounded upon the Washani Way (related to the Nez Perce faith called Seven Drum and the Yakama Washat), where the central belief was that the religion's prophets died and were resurrected to return with instructions for salvation. Smohalla's followers believed that a return to their own traditions was vital. Throughout the 1880s Smohalla challenged the legitimacy and foundations of the "progress" that was threatening indigenous lives and ways, contributing to a tradition of peaceful resistance.

In the lives of everyday people, spiritual traditions were kept alive and nurtured by song. Today, whether the song accompanies someone's work, guiding their hands or step, or whether the song is for healing or hunting—it is prayer. Traditional song is the link with the universe, the pulse of creation. Through the transformative quality of singing, the First People maintain spiritual communication. And by sensitive and disciplined living, the human spirit finds its place of harmony and balance with this time and place—this earth we call Mother.

Honored grandmother Vi [taqʷšəblu] Hilbert said, "The young people are finally referring to the songs as prayers. It makes me happy to hear them. . . . All the spiritually powerful songs that have ever been sung by our ancestors are out there, in the Universe. They come drifting down to us. Not everyone lives a life worthy to receive these songs."

One of the most significant aspects of the spiritual beliefs among many of Washington's indigenous people is the independent development of personal power and inner spirituality. As foreign to Euro-American settlers as Euro-American beliefs were to tribal peoples, Native beliefs were not recognized for the sophisticated systems they are. Formal gatherings and spiritual training are carried out in much different settings and time periods. They follow a different rhythm. The First People believe that humans are responsible for their own actions and that their activity directly affects the world they live in. An attitude of respect pervades personal development and guides interactions with others and the environment. Each person is expected to seek personal spiritual development. Bonds in the natural world with plant and animal realms provide guidance for living with integrity and balance. Ceremony is designed to provide part of this guidance.

It is also through ceremony that healing takes place. Respected elder Delores George from the Yakama Nation recalled that communities worked together to help restore balance and health to their members. "In an older time," she notes, "not more than a generation or two, Soup Dances were held as part of memorial, or honoring, activities for veterans. After other prayers, songs, or dances, a time would come to have soup served around the room. After the soup was eaten, those soldiers who had returned from battle would speak of their experiences: what the enemy had done to them, what they had done to the enemy. It was a healing time."

Oh, Those Boarding Schools

Music is a social adhesive providing a voice for love, for education, for healing, for welcome, and for farewell. Song provides people with a link to the environment, other people, and their spiritual essence. Many Native people have proudly re-counted their ancestral links: the band, tribe, ancestors; the birthplaces of aunts, uncles, cousins, and chiefs related to their offspring. These are chants, liturgies, for-ever etched in memory. When asked the right question, adults find themselves speak-ing their own history, chanting it the way they heard it as children. Complete histories are unlocked, summoning the person and all of their ancestors. To think about historical oral communication as a form of music and song is a key to under-standing the music and dance traditions of the Native people of Washington State. By interrupting those oral traditions other aspects of learning can also suffer, for ex-ample, the retention of material based on oral transmission. Boarding school inter-rupted this age-old way of teaching.

In 1893, education outside the tribal community was made mandatory for Na-tive children. This was many years before public education was required for United States citizens and thirty-one years before Native people were themselves considered citizens. Great effort on the part of the United States went into changing Native people into Christians; government-subsidized boarding schools were run by vari-ous churches to that end.

The approach to song and music in these schools was very different from what Native people understood. Many of the schools were run like military academies. A major goal was to erase every semblance of tribal life and values. The children were subjected to harsh scrubbings, their hair was cut off, and they were often forced to wear uniforms. They were punished for speaking their own languages. Girls were trained in "women's work" while boys were given training thought to prepare them for some technical or labor occupations. For some, the skills learned in the boarding schools made it possible for them to enter the labor force. On occasion, music pro-vided those skills, although the kind of music promoted in a boarding school was quite different from that enjoyed by children in their own homes.

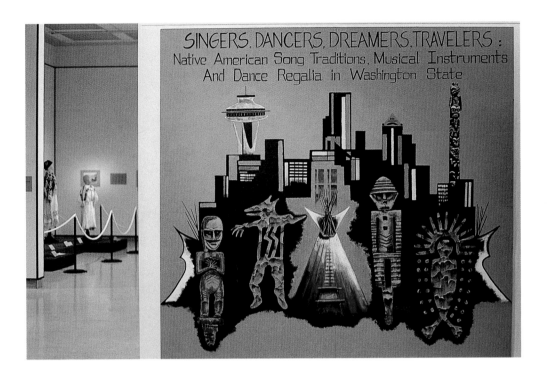

1. INTRODUCTORY PANEL by Gary Greene, Nez Perce, created for the 1992 Northwest Folklife Festival exhibit "Spirit of the First People." *Photograph by Roberta Haines*

2. MASK OF POOK-UBS, SPIRIT OF THE DROWNED WHALER.
Cedar, cedar bark, bear fur, horsehair. Made by Greg Colfax, Makah, 1991.
Loaned to the exhibit by The Legacy, Ltd. *Photograph by Ray Fowler*

This potlatch mask honors the spirit of a drowned whaler. The Makah tell of a whaling
crew that returned home to find the remains of their lost harpooner. His bones were
bleached white. In honor of his death, the crew had this mask made. Before whaling, they
danced to ask for protection. No whaler has died since from whaling in Neah Bay.

3. MASK. Alder, hair, abalone, paint. This mask is used during the Mask Dance
and the Dagger Dance. Made by John C. "Cal" Burch, 1988–89. Loaned to the
exhibit by the Snoqualmie Tribe. *Photograph by Ray Fowler*

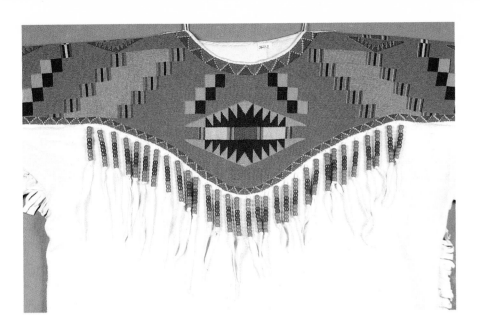

4. BEADED DRESS, PLATEAU. White buckskin, beads, geometric design.
Made by Lizzie Quintana, Spokane, ca. 1950s. Loaned to the exhibit by the
Cheney Cowles Museum. *Photograph by Ray Fowler*

5. TINKLER BAG. Made from cornhusk with tin tinklers. Loaned to the exhibit by the
Larry Jordan family, Colville Confederated Tribes. *Photograph by Ray Fowler*

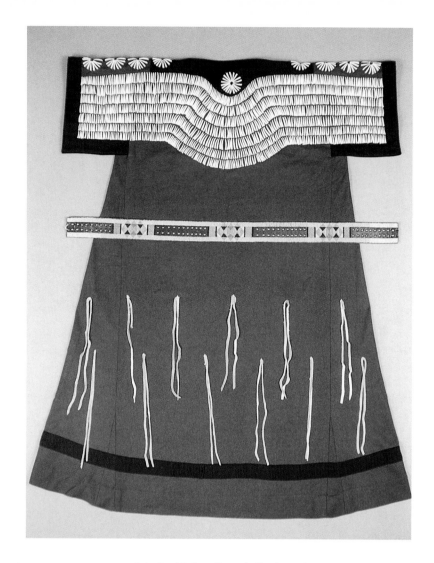

6. WING DRESS, PLATEAU. Wool, with dentalium shell yoke and smoked buckskin fringe. Reconstructed by Colleen Cawston, 1986; beaded belt made by Rodney Cawston, 1981. Loaned to the exhibit by the Cawstons, members of the Colville Confederated Tribes.

Photograph by Ray Fowler

Traditional regalia for dance and ceremony, wing dresses were developed by Plateau designers at the turn of the century. They retain a distinct preference for style while adapting to the new fabrics. Although beads were becoming popular, dentalium was a very rare, expensive treasure. These small shells were purchased by the string; the long ones were the most valuable.

7. BUCKSKIN SHIRT AND LEGGINGS, WITH HEADDRESS, SPOKANE. Buckskin, beads in geometric design; bald and golden eagle feathers in full-feather headdress, 1939–40. Loaned to the exhibit by the Cheney Cowles Museum. *Photograph by Ray Fowler*

Worn by Willie Andrews, Spokane Tribe, this southern Plateau style shirt is open down the front, with square-cut sleeves and fringe. The beaded strips on the arms, leggings, and shoulders are in a "lazy" overlay stitch that is formed by applying beads in short rows. These strips were attached to a separate piece of buckskin before being sewn onto the garment.

8. CEDAR BARK DRESS. Shredded red cedar bark, cloth. Made by Arlene Williams, Upper Skagit, 1986. Loaned to the exhibit by Tulalip Tribes Museum. *Photograph by Ray Fowler*

9. WOMAN'S PADDLE REGALIA AND HAIR HAT.
Regalia (*qua qua stinalwit*): green velvet, wood paddles, embroidery and sequin-accented roses. Hat (*seeatstin*): human hair, rhinestone trim. Regalia made by Bertha Visser, Debbie Johns, and Bruce-*subiyay* Miller, Twana; hat by Ray Krise, Twana, 1983. Loaned to the exhibit by Bruce-*subiyay* Miller, Skokomish/Twana. *Photograph by Ray Fowler*

Worn for the secret society blackface ceremony at the Coast Salish Winter Spirit Dance. These garments were formerly made of animal skin.

10. SCALLOP SHELL RATTLE. Made from eight scallop shells, feathers, cedar bark, metal, 1980s. Loaned to the exhibit by Helma Swan, Makah. *Photograph by Ray Fowler*

11. FOUR DIRECTIONS DRUM. Rawhide, wood. Made and loaned to the exhibit by Michael Rounds, Colville Confederated Tribes. *Photograph by Lou Corbett*

Cushman Trade School Band, Tacoma, Washington, ca. 1910.

Courtesy of Washington State Historical Society, Tacoma, Washington, neg. POR-1.04.032

Song Traditions
Serenades

A serenade was a song or melody for lovers, or, more generally, a "calling out" or invitation. Although we most often think of male performers, in eastern Washington, men and women serenaded each other. Mari Watters, a Nez Perce flute player, recalled that a young woman might sit outside in the warm summer moonlight and play melodies on her flute to the man who attracted her. Or a man might stroll through camp in the evening looking for those special eyes, that warm smile. When he found the right person, he might sing to her a while, accompanied by a gentle or provocative hand drum rhythm.

"In some camps," reminisced Delores George, "the teenagers had a more aggressive serenade for their friends. Some of the young boys held a rawhide skin between them to beat on like a drum. They went from camp to camp singing songs to bring other youngsters (especially their girlfriends) out to join their game. Sometimes they were given food or presents to send them on their way."

The Value of a Song

Around Puget Sound and on the Olympic Peninsula, song and music traditions have reached a state of refined formality. Songs and accompanying ceremonies, masks, and regalia are so prized that a formal system exists to regulate and protect their use. Owners of songs are proud of them and guard them carefully. Strict rules are enforced about the ownership, inheritance, and use of a song. At public ceremonies, official witnesses are chosen. Hank "Kwi Tlum Kadim" Gobin of the Tulalip Tribes notes that it is an honored responsibility to be called a witness. Witnesses must keep memory-record of the event, so that they can authenticate song ownership at a later date. They are paid for their wisdom and skill.

Ceremonies and political events often require the performance of specific songs. If the host does not own such a song, as Helma Swan of the Makah Culture and Research Center explains, the host must hire someone who does own the song. Before these songs are sung, their history is proclaimed, and how and when ownership was acquired is announced. In this way, the songs provide a tool for sharing historical, social, and political culture.

Voices from the Water

Historically, travelers to Puget Sound and along the Pacific Northwest coast arrived for gatherings by canoe. Songs from the canoes announced the arrival of each family and were greeted by songs of welcome from the shore. Canoes, even rooftops, were transformed into drums as those on the shore pounded a rhythm with oars to accompany their song. Today, welcome songs and dances are also performed by guests upon arrival by canoe.

Dance Regalia
Let's Dance

"In the old days," says Delores George, "the contests weren't organized the way they are today. The whole idea was to show particular dances and dancers to everyone else. The very skilled dancers would be honored. Their names would be called out and they would be recognized that way. And, because it is our custom to give gifts, the best dancers would be given gifts."

Large powwow-style gatherings have become popular places to meet new friends and become reacquainted with old ones in urban centers, like Seattle. Dancers compete with each other in categories of style, age, and dress. Dance contest committees decide what popular dances are attracting attention. These committees influence dress and dance styles nationwide.

Throughout the year there are other occasions for people to gather and renew friendships. Adeline Fredin, of the Colville Confederated Tribes' History Department, remembers that social dances provided opportunities for young people to dress up, show off, and get to know each other. Pairs of dancers joined the circle for the Owl Dance or the Rabbit Dance. Sometimes a circle of dancers formed for a Round Dance, giving everyone a chance to mix. Delores George remembers the fun of dances where a boy would tap one of a pair of girls on the shoulder as his choice for a dance partner. Similar "tag" dancing was common throughout the state.

Traditional Gathering

Powwows and celebrations do not have to be events for thousands of people. In fact, in many Native communities throughout Washington, more personal versions of

Suquamish Welcoming Ceremony. Second Annual Chief Seattle Days, Suquamish, Washington, 1912. *Courtesy of University of Washington Libraries, Special Collections Division, neg.* NA-1954

Clarissa Cawston and classmates dancing, 1992.
Photograph by Mike Bonnicksen; courtesy of Wenatchee World

these gatherings occur, cherishing the importance of community ceremony. Memorials are accompanied by song and feasting, stories, and reminiscences. Namings and the announcement of new dancers are similarly accompanied by music, prayers, gifts, and festivities.

At the powwow and celebrations where people gather in the summer and fall, activities include dances that are intertribal mixers, competition dances, demonstrations, and performances. There are also other activities that draw people together on these occasions through shared musical tradition. Perhaps the most popular of these are the gambling games, especially *slahal*, the stick or bone game. This game begins when one team matches the wagers of a second team. Players face each other behind parallel poles. Counting sticks are exchanged as the teams guess the position of the gaming pieces (bones). A large crowd often gathers behind the seated team players as powerful gambling songs, used to distract, intimidate, and taunt, are accompanied by the rousing beat of hand drums. The bone games are an arena for challenging, for gaming, and as with other aspects of Native life for those players who are masters, the power of the song is recognized as a nearly tangible force. Calling out, singing this force, invoking it for the team is the true essence of gambling. (See "The Origin of the Bone or Stick Game," Chapter 2.)

Voices Between Worlds: Masks and Face Paint

Mask making is a fine art on the Olympic Peninsula, especially for Makah dances, and is being revived in Puget Sound and the Cascade foothills. Makah masks represent animal figures and images from the other world. Family dance masks from Puget Sound, including those from Snoqualmie, Suquamish, and Tulalip recognized for their elemental symbolic form, are precise and clearly defined. Many represent human images in simple elegance. Others are realistic animal representations. On the other side of the state, among the eastern Washington Plateau peoples, vision-inspired face painting, animal heads, skins, and feathers are incorporated to honor and represent particular animal characteristics.

One of the goals of social dance is to combine expression and communication. An important aim in ceremonial dance is to achieve a transformation. Garments, masks, accessories, and paint are chosen to help each person achieve these goals. In ceremony, the community is transported through song and dance to another experience. The dancer, singer, and observer travel together as a community—sometimes to a place of rich experience—of dreams, of visions. (Plates 2 and 3)

Stick game, played at a gathering marking the removal of a tribal burial ground (cemetery), Colville Confederated Tribes, Kettle Falls, Washington, 1939.
Photograph by Wallace Gamble; courtesy of Cheney Cowles Museum, neg. L85-143.120

Plateau Regalia: Women's Wing Dresses

Buckskin dresses, shirts, skirts, and leggings have long been popular throughout eastern Washington. Durable and protective against the severe weather, the garments have become an institution in ceremonial and celebratory activities (Plate 4). A very popular dress was made of two deerskins tanned to a velvety softness. The skins were attached at shoulder and side seams with the tails folded down at the front and back neckline. Beadwork or shells were applied following the wavy contour around the tail. Many dressmakers today use this traditional undulating design whether or not they are working with two complete deerskins.

Blending Native and Euro-American styles, the "wing dress" was created around the turn of the century (Plate 6). A long-sleeved underdress of one fabric and pattern is worn with an overdress of a different pattern. The overdress reflects traditional preferences: unclosed arm seams and a yoke-style bodice. The yoke is sometimes decorated, especially when the dress is of heavier materials such as wool and velvet. The cotton version of this dress was worn for everyday activities and is still the choice among at least one generation of women. The garments were trimmed with scarves and necklaces. Women often wore headscarves or basketry hats and carried beaded or twined handbags (Plate 5).

In days past, women's outfits were two separate pieces: either a shirt worn with a skirt or a dress with shoulder straps worn under a short buckskin poncho. Called a "shoulder," this poncho might be completely covered with designs in beads or shells for ceremonial gatherings. It could be changed for one less ornately decorated for other occasions. "With the fringe they looked like a one-piece dress," notes Adeline Fredin. "I haven't seen this style for a long time but it's the way many women used to dress."

Plateau Regalia: Men's Wear

Men's ceremonial and dance regalia is often elaborately decorated with beads, porcupine quills, animal pelts, claws, hooves, and horn. Originally ornamented for serious occasions, councils, and ceremonies, the buckskin shirts and leggings reflect a man's relationships with his environment—spiritual, human, animal (Plate 7). The spirits of the animals are honored by the designs and accessories in the regalia. Dancing is a way to draw close to the spirit world and honor the skills, spirits, and characteristics of animal kinships.

Western Washington Regalia

The dance regalia worn by Native peoples of Puget Sound, the Olympic Peninsula, and the Pacific Coast of Washington makes creative use of every conceivable combination of fabric and material. Garment makers are guided by a traditional preference for a basic straight tunic derived perhaps from the straight woven cedar dress (Plate 8). Some early garments were made of skin. Today, many women's dresses, usually made of a lightweight fabric, are decorated with shells and fringe. Others are made of muslin with painted designs in red or black. Some ceremonial dresses were much heavier. These were made of wild goat or sheep wool (or a combination of both), wool tradecloth, or velvet.

Capes for Dancing

Capes are made from heavy material. Originally of cedar bark or wild goat wool, cape material has included wool, canvas, and various heavy-weight cottons. Today, weavers still produce beautiful blanket capes and shawls. The chill moist winters require several layers, and the clothing is designed to allow maximum comfort for the dancers. Fabric capes are painted or appliquéd with family crests (like coats of arms); and special dance steps are performed to fully display these designs. In some instances, buttons are applied to outline the crest. In the early days of trade with non-Native adventurers, a button was the equivalent of a full day's wages. They were thus quite valuable and maintain a place of importance as dance accessories.

Although button blankets are more usually associated with the nations of north Vancouver Island and Alaska, they are found among the traditional regalia on the Olympic Peninsula, worn primarily by the members of the Makah Nation. Canvas capes with traditional designs of the Puget Sound became popular in this area from about the 1920s or 1930s. Tribal groups borrow from each other and adapt styles to modern fabrics. Thus the Makah child might wear a cotton outfit with traditional designs painted on it, representing a woolen outfit she might have worn had she lived in an earlier era.

Paddle Regalia

Paddle regalia is worn for ritual dances (Plate 9). Each dress or tunic is decorated with uniquely patterned paddles. The beaded yokes and paddle designs help identify the dancers' membership. The hair headgear is sometimes called an ancestor hat and is made of human hair, often strands from the heads of relatives or ancestors. Another of the ritual societies wears regalia made from shredded cedar woven with wool, and it sometimes includes a tunic or dress and large rings of wrapped cedar bark.

Musical Instruments

In the spiritual traditions of western Washington, musical instruments are not ordinary tools for sound-making. Throughout the Puget Sound they represent the voices from the other world. Rattles and whistles are the most significant vessels of these spirit voices and are made and handled with reverence (Plate 10).

The simple elegance of the carved rattles found in the Puget Sound area characterizes a style of work becoming recognized throughout the coastal region of the state for its grace and simplicity. The forms are usually gently curved, although a few have flat surfaces in front. Handles are often wrapped. These bird rattles are an essential part of a dance, representing the particular bird honored in the song.

Drums provide the main support for song along the coast of Washington. The sound begins on a personal and small scale with hand clapping. In older days the sound built to deep echoing vibrations created by rhythmic beating on rooftops with poles or oars, transforming the entire longhouse into an enormous drum. Hand drums are the most common and expressive instrument accompanying dancers and singers today. Many singers play their own drums, often decorated with personal symbols (Plate 11).

ROBERTA HAINES, a member of the Moses Band of the Wenatchee tribe (Colville Confederated Tribes), curated "Singers, Dancers, Dreamers, Travelers," the "Spirit of the First People" exhibit. She was previously co-curator of the state centennial exhibit "A Time of Gathering: Native Heritage in Washington State." Ms. Haines is currently a Ph.D. candidate in political science at the University of California, Los Angeles.

Seeds of Our Ancestors

Growing Up in the Skokomish Song Tradition

BRUCE-*SUBIYAY* MILLER

"I'm the 15th one in my family"

We Coast Salish people were trained not to rush into immediate conversation during visits or meetings. We were to show courtesy to the ancestors who dwelt within us (our guardian spirits) by silently enjoying each other's company, thus allowing our spiritual beings to communicate. After a polite amount of time had passed, casual formalities were observed and a mutual comfort zone was established. It was then that the conversation began.

When I was a child, we adhered to this practice. But anthropologists and linguists would come out and, as soon as they walked in the door, start asking questions. They got impatient with our elders, who wanted to observe the correct etiquette and take the proper amount of time to respond.

The process of allowing the ancestors to visit involves a lot of visualization. It is like letting your thoughts drift through times past. You look at the visitors and remember the times you have spent together. If they are strangers, you allow your senses to facilitate the silence by feeling what kind of emanations they give off. Mental images and emotional feelings mix before the verbal conversation starts. It is a way to purify and open the path for communication to begin.

Now that we have met, let us speak of songs.

Bruce-*subiyay* Miller. *Photograph by Jill Sabella; courtesy of Washington State Arts Commission*

ACCORDING TO THE TEACHINGS OF OUR ELDERS, SONGS EXISTED before the spoken language. Our traditions teach that songs were given to the human people by the bird people to express what we now call emotions. It was through the expression of these emotions that our people could release pent-up pressures and frustrations, or feel great joy. Through these songs, they were also able to express their unity, as well as their contentment and serenity. The songs allowed the people to purify themselves by releasing all these emotions.

Along with the songs came the gestures and movements of dance. The movements of dance and the emotions of song tell a story that allows us to convey our feelings and important messages to others. Our people today retain the "seeds of the ancestors," the emotions and intuitions of our heritage. If you watch young children, you will see that they sing on their own before they can speak. This is the way they begin to relate experiences or interact with each other. These are the seeds of our ancestors showing themselves in the people of today.

We see the importance of songs in all aspects of our lives: in our everyday life, in our ritual life, and in the national unity of our people. Countries have national anthems. Schools have alma maters. Organizations have secret songs. Tribes have flag songs, which honor their people of valor. Songs are a part of religious gatherings. They give us hope and inspiration or serenity and peace. The traditions, rituals, dances, stories, and courting and funeral customs of our people have been handed down from generation to generation through songs. The continuance of these ritual and traditional songs, in modern times, gives us a sense of well-being. Songs are a part of every cell in our body and have been from the beginning of time.

Ritual has always been an important part of our lives. Tradition teaches that, after the songs, certain rituals were given to our people. The people were told to revere the animals, who also have rituals that add meaning to their own lives.

Shuy *(Spiritual Foundation)*

Songs and the rituals and movements that go with them form a part of our culture that we call *shuy*, the spiritual foundation of our lives. It is the thing that gives us a true sense of well-being. When we have a *shuy* we can sit down, relax, let our minds drift, and be in harmony with the universe. When rituals are capsized (changed or eliminated), we become out of balance. We say, "I must have gotten out on the wrong side of the bed" or "I'm out of tune." Many phrases used in popular culture relate to the sense of a natural rhythm that we can feel within ourselves. "We're out of step," "We're off the beat," and "We're out of harmony" are examples.

Telling the Stories of Our Lives

In the Puget Salish culture we have "spirit songs" that are part of our private religious practices. These are songs that symbolically tell the stories of our lives, and therefore teach us to enjoy ourselves, to achieve the *shuy*, the spirit within. This is also connected with the rituals of life and death. When a person has a terminal illness or is simply in failing health because of old age, we have what are called "the escorts." The escorts go to these people and get them to reminisce about their memories from the earliest ones all the way to the present time. Thus they can leave this earth unhindered and dance or float off into the next world without having to struggle to stay here. In the teachings, this verbal dialogue of memoirs is also the song of the dying person's life. By being able to relate this song, the person is able to go, without losing the rhythm, into the next world.

Even though these memoirs do not necessarily incorporate actual singing, they can. During this time, many elders who have not yet sung songs from their childhood will say, "This is what we sang when we were children," and they will do these little dances, which resemble physical exercises.

Songs for Physical Fitness

Physical fitness was very important to our old people. They made it into games and songs, and they had various dances that used what we now call muscle groups—small and large groups, rhythms and responses. The songs and percussion accompaniments incorporated squatting movements like a duck walking, or jumping and turning and twisting motions. The singer related the story of the Snipe Dance, or the story of how Raven was humiliated when he was bragging about being the greatest archer (and how Skate Fish, which is a large and gamey fish, overcame Raven's challenge). All these stories have little songs and dances that incorporate movements and twists.

Smustix^W *(Seeds of the Ancestors)*

Songs tell a story. They tell a story of the sadness of a people. They tell a story of the rejoicing and long journeys in the ancient days when the people were finding a place that would be theirs on the face of the earth. Through songs our ancestors live to this day, because as we sing these ancient family songs, they come to life for another generation. In that way these ancient songs, the very old songs, allow us to retain the seeds of our ancestors, this *smustix*^{W}.

Spelatch *(The Capsizing)*

Song is important not only to us as Salish people, but to all the people of the world, because at the beginning of time we were all one people. We all carry remnant characteristics of that time. *Spelatch* (the time of assimilation and treaty making) turned everything as we knew it upside down. Life as our ancestors knew it ceased to exist. The people fell into disarray and lost their *shuy*.

The first capsizing of the world was when human beings came into existence and took the stewardship of the earth away from the animal people. For the animal people, everything as they knew it turned upside down.

When the Puget Salish culture came to be decimated, everything they had known that gave them security, the knowledge of their ancestors' songs and ceremonies, was pulled out from under them. They were *spelatched*. Everything was turned upside down again. It was like a shipwreck where everyone was trying to find something to cling to, to save their lives. For a great many, what they clung to was alcohol, and the outcome was a short, miserable life. Many turned to acculturation. Many turned to Christian religions in an effort to find a new *shuy*—a firm place to stand again in the midst of that capsized world. For most of these people that only led to more *spelatch*, because it meant they had to cast aside any mention of their ancestral ways, which were considered creations of the devil. The things that they venerated, that gave them their vital life force and their strength for survival, suddenly were condemned as evil. But many of our people were afraid to cast away these beliefs, because we were told that when we lost the teachings of our ancestors, we would wander the world as faceless people in the crowd of humanity, with no foundation, no roots, no strength to survive. Many families kept these traditions alive in secret or seclusion. Many just handed down bits and pieces, which are the seed potatoes of those old ways. You can cut part of a potato off and it will regenerate into another potato. The bits of knowledge of our ancestral ways—which here in the Northwest were so thoroughly suppressed by the U.S. government and the Christian missionaries—began to sprout again in the 1920s as our people continued to go back and forth to what is now called Canada to participate in spirit dancing. Through this "smokehouse network" we were able to preserve those portions of our traditional life. We still partake of them today.

Learning twaduq *Song Traditions*

Our songs, stories, and legends contain many metaphors that are difficult to translate. The mention of a particular characteristic in a song or story implies, to those who are familiar with the story of this animal or thing, the full analogy of the song. Also, our sense of humor involves knowledge of these traditional stories, legends, and songs; thus interpretation of the language has been difficult for those who have not learned all the legends, songs, or stories first.

The way we learned songs was by listening to the elders. As children, my brothers and sisters and I were required to go to my great-grandmother's house. We went, not in the daytime, but just as dusk began. My great-grandmother, who was a tiny person, would sit there with a cane and wait until we all were quietly gathered in front of her before beginning to tell the stories. She would sing the songs that went with the stories. The smaller children just had to listen. The older ones had to respond with the word "*Hamakay!*" meaning "Oh, it is so!" or as the Christians would say, "Amen, Amen!"

Then somewhere during the story, my great-grandmother would stop and pretend to try to remember what came next (it was a test). One of the older children would have to say, "*Kaya* [grandmother], this is what they did," and then relate the next part of the story. After a while, Kaya would pick up the story again. When she got to the song part, "*Ah, dah dah* [my goodness], I can't remember," she would exclaim, and she would sit there in a feigned state of confusion until one of the older kids would say, "They sang this, Grandma." After the song, she would ask, "What would they do when they sang that?" That was the cue to do the dance movement. Many of the dances were easy to do sitting down. They were very simple. I remember this from my earliest childhood because we children had to participate as soon as we were able to walk.

Then there were the elders for whom this storytelling was their livelihood in old age. Some had lost all of their children during the influenza epidemics. Some were destitute (*hawoe*) in the eyes of the white man. They were old people who no longer had children of their own. They still had cattail mats and old-style Salish blankets. On a winter evening you would hear a knock at the door and one of them would be standing there. Everybody knew they would visit for two or three days. They would roll their mats out in front of the fireplace in the house of my grandparents. My grandparents would bring them food and everyone would sit around and be "quiet," as was the custom.

When the time was right, Dewey Leschi, a descendant of Chief Leschi of the

Nisqually, to whom we are related, would begin to tell the stories. The twist in his stories was that he went into elaborate descriptions of the dress and customs of the characters. They were dressed as the finest people in his youth would have been dressed, with silk top hats and swallow-tailed coats, and gowns, and their hair fixed and twisted with ribbons. He described the Indians and animals as dressed in that way and portrayed how they curtsied and bowed. He had adapted all these descriptions to his own style of storytelling. I got a hint of how creative people can be. He always expressed things so graphically.

Later, not long before he died, I asked him why he adapted the stories. He explained that the young children didn't have any way of relating to the old cedar-bark clothes, the mountain-goat blankets, and the rituals. So in order to keep the stories alive, he had to adapt them to things that children could visualize. In his stories the canoes became horseless carriages.

Later on, in research that I was doing, I discovered some contemporary Mayan tales in which biblical stories were similarly transformed. In one of these, instead of Jesus arriving on a white donkey on Palm Sunday, he comes on a four o'clock train. I saw that some of the Mayans used that same kind of creativity in telling their stories. But the ancient story line remained the same.

Most of our stories had songs in them. The old people say, "You have to sing the most important teaching of a story for children to remember it." I laughed with my school staff one day when we realized that this is what television commercials do. They give you the most crucial message in a jingle. These important song lines were sometimes very short, maybe only four words or sometimes four lines at the most. They were simple, like a commercial jingle. They stayed with the child because a song will stay with you all of your life, and a verbal history lesson will not. If you were to take the most important part of that history lesson and sing it to the children, and make a game of it, they would remember it forever.

Singing our songs also builds a person's character and ability to speak in public. In the old days, participation was a keynote of survival. You had to jump in with a group of people and participate. Songs allowed you to lose that bashfulness and sing along with the other kids and play the group games like tug-of-war.

In the army, songs with cadence are used in a similar way to change and assimilate people. Many people who go into military service are shy and reserved. The military training tries to beat that out of them physically and mentally. Through army songs and rigid exercises you are made to come into rhythm with others as you holler out the cadence.

Songs help us traditional people remember the stories that are such an important part of oral traditions. My great-grandfather didn't speak English very well, but he would often talk about how reading made us lazy. He didn't know how to read. He had to remember everything, so his mind had to be very retentive. He said that written words were just a shadow of the spoken word. You have to add the vocal interpretation, the inflection, the projection, the diminishing and raising of the voice that bring information to life.

Song Ownership

In the Pacific Northwest some songs are personal property. In the old days it was felt that anyone who did not have some way of participating in the survival of the village would have no personal empowerment. Those who had no song to sing were considered poor. But if their family owned a song that was necessary in the sequence of a ritual, then regardless of whether they were poor or wealthy, they were important in the spiritual life and the well-being of the village.

These songs and legends at one time were of greater importance because they were the wealth of our people. Many have forgotten or never learned of this wealth. The songs and legends told us of life at the beginning. They were our equivalent of Genesis, Exodus, and Leviticus in the Bible. Some songs were family-owned, and some went freely to whomever was told the story. Some songs were spontaneous, particularly songs of basket makers, canoe carvers, and paddle makers. That was part of the personal power of those people. Sometimes they would give the songs to their apprentices to sing.

The songs were one of the seeds that really perpetuated the strength of the stories. Songs that certain families owned were used in different rituals. Some were used in secret society functions with various kinds of rattles and masks. Songs were used with the spreading of the feathers on the floor of the longhouse before important work, and with the casting of the red ochre to bless things.

When you put all these songs of the old days together you had songs of the uniform makers, the paint throwers, the feather throwers, songs of the people who give the first bath to the newly initiated, songs of the people who bless an impending journey. All these songs were building blocks of a nation. Each component was important in making up the whole.

Today, we have family songs that can be publicly shared by other families. These are specific songs that belong to family lines. Other people may sing them, but it is bad etiquette to sing them unless the family who owns the song begins it first. Then you may join in with them. Sometimes an elder might tell you a legend and the songs that go with it, thereby allowing you to keep alive that story and song for to-day's children.

Through this hundred years of *spelatch* some families have become very cautious about sharing songs. We've had people (anthropologists) come through the village who have recorded family stories, copyrighted them, and then refused to allow them to be used or republished by the original owners.

The Twana Dancers

We have given our family songs to the group we call the Twana Dancers. They are the ones who keep these songs alive today. Some we have not recorded yet, but we will. Those are nonreligious songs for children. Most have dance and exercise movements.

We started the Twana Dancers in 1975 for the Bicentennial of the United States. Within my extended family groups, we were discussing how many of the Coast Salish people were dancing around in imitation of the Plains Indians wearing such Plains regalia as bustles and roaches, and projecting an image of a Native people that had nothing to do with our own culture. We agreed that it was the "Hollywood Indian image." We thought this was very sad, but nobody was doing anything about it. So we decided there was a need for us to share some of our family lineage for the good of our Salish people. We got a small grant from the Washington State Arts Commission to get material to make some of the dance uniforms, and that was the beginning.

The Twana Dancers are now their own independent group. In that short span of time we produced dancers who are third-generation members. When we started the troupe, the dancers' ages ranged from two to ninety-two.

The development of our group gave focus to the issues that can arise between tribal traditionalists and Christians. The ninety-two-year-old member of the group had retained much traditional knowledge from her childhood. When she became a Christian woman, she was taught that this knowledge was a tool of the devil, and that she must not pass it on. But after watching the Twana Dancers, she felt it was important that these aspects of our culture be preserved. So some of our dances came from her. She decided that they didn't come from the devil.

Spirit Songs

In addition to the family songs, there are songs that are very individual. Our people believe that everyone has a spirit song. Some seek them in their spirit questing. You are empty without a personal song. It is this song that allows you to express your greatest joys or release your deepest sorrows. If we walk through life without a personal song, we will have a void within us. One day we may hear a commercial jingle or a rock-and-roll song, and a few notes of that song will stick with us. The harder we try not to sing or hum that melody, or tap a finger or foot to the rhythm, the stronger the urge to react to it becomes. The old people said that these melodies contain the notes of your spirit song and they have awakened your soul. Your soul keeps repeating them. But an hour later you might forget the little jingle you were humming because the song has fulfilled its temporary purpose, and your spirit no longer needs to hear it. When you find your spirit song, all the internal things that have been bothering you, the frustrations and sadness that you haven't consciously dealt with, will subside through the healing notes of that song.

Songs Connected with Games

Of the songs connected with games, the bone game songs are the most popular. In this game, one team tries to guess the location of certain marked sticks or bones hidden in the hands of members of the opposing team. (See a related story at the end of this chapter.) I have been singing in a bone game group for over thirty years. That's my social life, and the social life of all those who participate in the bone game circuit, which generally starts in May, when the salmonberries bloom.

Not all who come to these games are gamblers. Some just come to sit, or to visit. Some are intense gamblers; some bet only a couple of dollars. Most of those who travel in the circuit are the same people with whom we spend all winter doing spiritual practices, such as spirit dancing, in the longhouse.

The Power of Story and Song

One of the best ways of showing the power of song and story is by relating a story. I have one that illustrates this.

An old woman was holding a Chinook medicine dance that turned out to be five days long. As the one who ran the dance, she had to sing last. There were many adolescents who were asked to attend to such duties as keeping the fire going. Probably about four in the morning on the fifth day, she had them wheel her over in her wheelchair from the bed where she was lying. She began to sing her medicine song. She sang the first chorus.

In keeping with the structure of Chinook dance songs, she then stopped and related what she had received spiritually after that verse. She said, "It makes me so angry. The young people in there throwing the people around like that. Treating those people with disrespect." She went on about how they were treating these people like they were no one, slamming them down. She said:

> You might wonder what people I'm talking about. I'm talking about those you call dishes and plates in there. In my youth those were like people. They fed us when we were sick, they fed us when we rejoiced, they fed us when we were in sorrow. They nourished us. And each one of them was important, because each one of those people came into my life at a different point. I received some of them at my wedding. Some of them came to me at a loved one's memorial. Each one had a story of its life. When I was a young girl we were taught to treat these people with respect, and to take care of them because they were somebody important. Now we live in a society that no longer treats these people with respect. They slam them down on the counter, throw them down in the sink, chip them, treat them with disrespect. And they wonder why the families are falling apart.

Then, after she sang again, she started her second commentary:

> And those other people, they allow their children to jump up and down in them and to kick them. They degrade them when they become ragged and broken down. They throw them out of their lives. These people are our furniture. When I was young we didn't have much furniture, but each piece was important. Like the old chair at my house, it's been with me since I first married in the early 1890s. It held me with my first child. It comforted me when my first child died. It rejoiced when my grandchildren came. It held my weary body when I came home from long journeys so my mind could drift and remember all that was. But now as soon as these people get old and sag a little bit, the young people want to throw them out and replace them. Just like us old people, they want to put us in old folks' homes and separate us from the family because we're old and useless.
>
> This person we live in, they slam the doors, break the windows, curse one another, stab each other with words. We call this person our house, our home. Now, we wonder why the young people are the way they are today. You look around, you see the old people who allowed the young people to jump up and down on their furniture, to throw the dishes around. When they get old, their children are going to treat them the same. They're going to put them in old folks' homes. They're not going to respect them anymore because they are old and worn out and they are useless. They strive to fill their kitchens with beautiful sets of matching dishes that have no history, no spiritual quality. And when these dishes become old or chipped they are given away, thrown out because they have no meaning. When their furniture becomes saggy, old, and has no meaning, they allow their children to jump up and down on it and then they throw it out.
>
> All the children of these people are the reasons society is like it is today. They cannot respect one another. To have respect you have to start out with the simplest things.

She talked about her dance cane:

It is just an old stick. This dance stick has been with me since I was thirteen years old. It's been with me through all the joys and sorrows of my life. When I stood on the highest mountains I leaned on it and we beheld what lay before us. When I drifted in memory it shared this and held me.

Too many people today, when they see me walk around with this old stick, they want to give me a nice new cane that makes different lengths. Some of them have four legs on the bottom. But this stick is me. This stick is my life. When I was thirteen years old I sang that this stick would be with me for my entire life. I was told as a young girl, how I took care of this stick would be how I took care of my people. Now we live in a society of people who can't take care of each other, because they have never been able to take care of the simplest things that lie around them. You are the way you treat your house, your dishes, the things around you.

She saw these things around us as if they were with us from the beginning of time. She said that families are dysfunctional now because homes are no longer sacred. You never argued or belittled each other in traditional homes. If that ever came about, you knew to go outside. Now, people scream and yell at each other in their homes. That disrespect has nowhere to go but right down to the children. When you go outside it can blow away. She pointed out that people today don't respect the little things. She said:

You can't have a cohesive society. You have old folks' homes, you have street people, you have people wandering, abandoned. You have husband-beaters, wife-beaters, child-beaters. You have incest and all the things that destroy society today.

Intertwined with this narrative, she sang her medicine song.

The Origin of the Bone or Stick Game

I'm going to tell the story of the bone, or stick, game—an activity that continues today among many Indian tribes. Here on the coast we call this game slahal. *Across the Strait of Juan de Fuca it is called* lahal *(meaning bones). East of the Cascades it is called the stick game. It is through this game that we received the right to eat the flesh of the animals and to use their songs for guardian spirit songs. This game is also supposed to replace the wars that caused bloodshed among the Indian nations.*

The bone, or stick, game is an intertribal gambling activity played throughout Washington State. It is a guessing game played with two sets of bones, one of which is marked. Two teams compete standing or sitting opposite each other. One side chooses two players to conceal the bones in their hands, and the other side guesses in which of the four hands the two unmarked bones are hidden. Long wooden tally sticks are kept or relinquished to count the scores for each team. The hiding team sings and drums to provide spiritual strength to the team members and distract the guessing team. This form of gambling continues as a popular recreational activity, but is also played to test the spiritual power of the thoughts and songs of the participants.

Long ago, when humans and animals were still able to talk to one another, they were given rules by the Creator. The animals were the first people. They were given the rules for learning how to survive in this land—for learning how to go through the hardships, joys, and frustrations of life. Through their sagas came the teachings for the human beings who were created later. The animals were given laws to protect them from the four seeds of destruction: greed, lust, hate, and jealousy.

All the animals were given the equivalent of national costumes, to identify them by groups or tribes. Each of the animal nations had a song that identified it, and each had a location in which it was to live. When human beings were created, they were told to observe the animals and to learn, through watching them, their laws and behavior and the repercussions that they would face if these laws were broken. If humans obeyed the laws, the weather would stay warm all year round, the food plants would grow in abundance, and there would be no sickness anywhere in the land. Everyone would grow and thrive.

But as time went on, the humans began to forget the promises they had made to the Creator. They forgot the Huckleberry Feast, the Salmon Feast, the First Elk

Bruce-*subiyay* Miller at a stick game, Northwest Folklife Festival, 1992.
Photograph by Lou Corbett; courtesy of Northwest Folklife

Ceremony, and the Cedar Ceremony. Because food was abundant, they forgot to give thanks for each day's bounty. Then they began to desire each other's mates. They began to covet another tribe's territory. They began to copy each other's way of dressing. These things caused much jealousy and anger among the tribes. Soon anger flared into hate and the tribes began to war.

The Creator was angry at the breaking of the laws and cast hardship upon the land. He poisoned the salt water, dried up the fresh water, and stopped the life-giving rain. The food began to disappear. But still the people fought one another. Soon they began to starve, because there was no more food.

The humans were defenseless creatures, for they had been given no special talents. They had no claws, no fur, no beaks with which to defend themselves. They were at the mercy of the animal people, who found them easy prey. One by one, the tribes became extinct.

You could see the people's bones scattered about the prairie. Other tribes became so small that there were only a few members left. Soon the people began to eat one another. The strong preyed on the weak, and fear ravaged the land. One day parents might be cuddling a child, the next day devouring it. Or the child might be stronger and might prey on its elders just to survive.

There came a time when there were just a few elders left who remembered the days when the laws were obeyed and everyone lived in harmony. These elders called the animals and the people together to work out a truce. They said, "Let's go to the mountain. There is one called the Creator who made all of this. Let us go and call for his aid."

Word was sent throughout the land for all the peoples to meet at the mountain. From the smallest to the largest, they began to journey toward the mountain from the prairies, forests, rivers, and beaches. On their way they passed the bones of those who no longer lived. There was a great murmur among them: "What will we ask the Creator for? What will the Creator give us?" They were tempted to kill each other along the way for food, but they restrained themselves. At last, those who remained were gathered on the mountain.

Together they called for the Great Spirit to answer them, to take the spell off the land, and to give them food again. The Creator answered by saying, "Look in all directions from where you stand, and tell me what you see." They looked out on the prairie and saw the bones of animals and people strewn in all directions. They also saw the bones of the dead and dying trees.

The Creator said to one animal person, "Go out on the prairie and bring me back four bones." He told one of the human people, "Go into the forest and bring me

Stick game, Neah Bay, 1940s–1950s. *Photograph by J. W. Thompson; courtesy of Yakama Nation Museum, neg.* CO-2892

Yakama stick game, 1940s–1950s.

Photograph by J. W. Thompson; courtesy of Yakama Nation Museum, neg. CO-3109

the bones of those trees." When this was done, the Creator asked for the four bones and marked them in two sets. He said, "There will be one bone with no marking on it to represent women. There will be one that will be decorated to represent men. Without both male and female, life cannot continue."

The Creator then told them that a game would be played. He explained the rules: "Scores will be kept with the bones of the trees. They will be marked in two pairs. The war chief will give one side the advantage of an extra stick. Whoever wins the first guess for the kick stick will start the game. The losers will be food for the winners until the end of time."

Immediately all the animals joined on the same side. They alone had spirit songs. On the other side were the human beings, who had nothing. They situated themselves to play. The animals were the first to hide the sticks. The humans pointed and missed. Now the humans had to hide the sticks, and the animals pointed and guessed correctly.

Having won the first guess, the animals were given the sticks, and the game began. The animals passed out the sets of sticks and began to sing their bone game songs. The humans made their guess by pointing toward the outside hands. They missed, so they had to throw two scoring sticks over to the animals. The humans tried it again, this time pointing to the inside hands, and they lost two more sticks to the animals. Soon the animals were pointing to one tribe of humans and saying, "These humans are going to be our food until the end of time."

The humans began to grow desperate. They pointed two more times. They continued to point until there were only two scoring sticks left. All that the humans could see were the animals bearing down upon them, choosing their food until the end of time. The humans huddled together and prayed to the Great Spirit for help. They vowed to keep alive the Huckleberry Ceremony, the Salmon Ceremony, the First Elk Ceremony, and the Cedar Ceremony. They vowed to keep alive the laws against the four seeds of destruction. They prayed until their prayer was heard. The Creator answered their prayers by giving them songs. He granted them the right to sing the songs of the animals. When they did this, they began to get the sticks back.

The animals pointed and missed. Then the humans sang again. The animals pointed and missed once more. The animals were down to one stick, and they began to look at one another. They began to look at the humans who now had great courage. They began to look at the mountain, the forest, and the prairie. Just as the animals made their last point and missed, they threw the stick across and fled to all directions of the world. The mountain goats fled to the mountain, the deer fled to the prairie, the salmon leaped into the river, and the snakes crawled away in the grass.

The rabbits hid in the underbrush and the grizzly bears went to the outer edge of the rugged mountains. They fled to the forest and the woods and to all the places where the animals live today.

To this day, we humans still eat the animals that we chose for our food. For our people, it was the salmon. From that time on, we retained the right to eat the animal and to quest for, and sing, the guardian spirit songs of the animal. From that time on, this game has been played to replace war. This is the origin of the stick game.

BRUCE-*subiyay* MILLER is a noted artist, ceremonial leader, and teacher from the Skokomish Nation. As a boy, profoundly influenced by his grandparents and his great-grandmother, he started to learn the traditions and knowledge of his family and culture. Tribal leaders taught him weaving, tribal oral traditions, history, and genealogy, and his family's ancient herbal knowledge. Today, *subiyay* is a recognized master of the Twana and Coast Salish art traditions, including carving and basket weaving, and his work is widely exhibited. In 1992 he received a Governor's Ethnic Heritage Award. On the importance of maintaining his culture, he recently commented, "To be without your culture is to be lost. It is like having all the food in the world, but none of it fulfills your hunger."

Cliff Sijohn at Northwest Folklife Festival, 1992.
Photograph by Lou Corbett; courtesy of Northwest Folklife

The Circle of Song

CLIFF SIJOHN

". . . So listen to your heart. Listen to your heart talk. Because it will tell you the truth. If you always talk with your heart, you'll always have clean hands. My grandmother taught me that, so I give that to you today."

Circle of Song

I've been asked to describe our song traditions and what they mean to me. Trying to do this in just a few words is very difficult. There's so much to tell. It would be like saying, "In twenty-five minutes tell me about your Bible and every story that's inside of it, and what it means, and where did it come from? How important is it? What does it sound like when you read it? What does this mean? What does that mean?"

How could you begin to interpret the Bible in twenty-five minutes? But that's the kind of thing we are sometimes asked to do as Indian people. We are asked to define our culture, to tell about all our songs, in a few minutes.

The process of talking about our songs is difficult for other reasons. These songs are so important to us that we don't like to have them analyzed or recorded. When we made the film *Circle of Song*, it took me almost six months to convince my father that it was important for him to allow me to include our songs in it.

It's important for us to retain our culture and our heritage, to sing and remember these songs. We must have them in our hearts—not on a tape, but in our hearts. But now the tribes are using tapes, and things like that, for teaching in their tribal schools.

Song to us is like the Bible. The eagle is also like the Bible to us, and so is the salmon. All of this is important for understanding the hearts of Indian people.

When most non-Indian people hear our songs, those are generally songs that belong to everybody—intertribal songs that you hear at powwows and public gatherings, songs that are passed around for us to take part in. The sacred songs are not meant to be heard by the general public. Those are for other places.

I've been living with our music all my life. My first memory was of songs sung by my grandfather. When I was a child we'd be in a building or in a longhouse or teepee, and I would sit by my grandmother. I remember lying behind her legs—lying sideways and looking out and seeing her moccasins and seeing the dancers late at night. I would go to sleep hearing song. When my children were born and my brother's children were born, and they were handed to their grandmother, she didn't say, "Oh, what a beautiful baby." The first thing that came out of her mouth and into the ears of that little person was song—our songs, our family's songs.

So the importance of songs to Indian people comes from the heart. When you look at all the beautiful things that Indian artists have made, like buckskin dresses, beadwork, and baskets, there is something you need to remember: when those dresses and baskets were made by our grandmothers and grandfathers, song was a part of each creation.

As a young person, I learned how to dance in the mountains. Every late summer or fall we'd go into the mountains to pick huckleberries. But we would go up there for a week or two, not just an afternoon. One time we stayed in teepees with our grandmother. Sure, we had a pickup to get us and our things up there, but we stayed in a teepee. And in the morning, the first thing I woke up to was a song—the wake-up song that my uncle was singing. From birth to death, there's a song. It's like marks on a clock, with a song for every point on the circle: for waking up, for being born, for becoming a man, for being in love, for marriage, for an addition to the family. There are welcoming songs, songs for learning your dances, songs for war dances, songs for being a warrior, battle songs, songs to taunt your enemy, and so on until, finally, the time comes for a death song.

Where do these songs come from? Well, we don't go to the Circle-K [convenience store] and buy them. And we don't go to the music store and buy sheet music to learn them. It's all oral history handed down. But there's another way the songs come to Indian people: they are delivered to us.

They are delivered to us by the messengers of the Great One. In the Bible—angels. For us, the messengers are the Owl, the Eagle, the birds, the Fish, the Ant, the Little Mouse, the Weasel, and so on. We don't pick where songs come from—they come to us. They come to us in the sweatlodge. They come to us in visions when we go into the mountains. That's why they are so sacred. And that's why, when we talk about songs, we talk about copyrights and we talk about handing them down and protecting them. Someone might say, "Well, what's the big deal?" The big deal is that the songs come from inside of us, and they are retained there for all of our lives.

It's like your grandmother putting a necklace around your neck when you are born and saying, "Your grandmother hangs this upon you. Don't ever take it away!" Because when you die the song will go with you into the next world. There your people will know you because you'll be able to sing their song. Your ancestors, the ones that have gone ahead of you, will recognize you because when you cross that creek you can sing that song, and someone will hear it and call out, "Somebody's coming! It's so-and-so. . . . It's so-and-so's grandson, he's coming!"

I tell non-Indian people to keep that in mind: when our people sing, it's like going to a communion with the Great Spirit. When Indian people sing, their songs come from inside their hearts, just as when Christians kneel down to pray. And we can do this anywhere. We can go outside and sing in the morning when we wake up, or in the evening when we go to bed. That's the circle of song.

I try to stress to people that our songs are like prayers. When non-Indians hear the drum beating and see the dancers, they often say, "Wow, it's so pretty! What beautiful dancers!" I tell them, "Don't look upon it as a show. That offends us. We're not entertainers. We come to share something with you." Listen to the song. Each song is unique and different. Each is a prayer. The dancers are praying. Indian people pray when they dance.

I try to help people understand that the Great Spirit appeared to Indian people too, just as he did to Mohammed, or Moses, or Peter. He told us: "You are all going to be here. You are all going to speak different languages, different tongues. But the one thing that will hold you together as a people is song. That is why I gave you that. And I give you the sweatlodge over here. That is how I will deliver it to you, so that you will see it with your heart first, not with your eyes."

Singing a Song on a Vietnam Battlefield

When I was a young man, I served in Vietnam. Some 80,000 Indian people served in Vietnam, more per capita than any ethnic group in this country. Let me tell you how song affected me over there. It was in a place a long way from here, a long time ago, but it seems like only a few minutes ago that it happened. This is not a war story— this is a story about song.

The enemy had come up and they had almost wiped us out, almost to a man. There were only five of us left. Everybody else was dead. I could hear the enemy all around us, and I knew I was not going to see another sunrise. I knew that! I knew I wasn't going to see my father again, or my mother, or my brother. So I did the only thing that came into my mind.

A song came into my mind, and I thought I was going crazy. In the midst of all these horrible things that were happening, people dropping here and there, a song came to me. And I had a feeling of calmness, because then I knew—I knew—the enemy was not going to take me. He wasn't going to take my life. I could see him, I could hear him, but he wasn't going to take me, not that day. He might destroy my body, but he wouldn't take *me*.

So I climbed up on some sandbags that were parked there, and stood up there in front of all of them, and I stripped down—took everything off—and I sang my death song. "Come and get me, enemy! If you are strong enough—come and get me! Take me—now! Do it now while I sing my song, because I'm on my way. I'm going away. You will not touch me. You cannot take me when I have my song." And I sang my song and the enemy stopped advancing. Of the other four people who were left, one, an Indian from Arizona, was my good friend. The other three were non-Indians. And they stared at me, except for my friend, who was shot and wounded. He was lying there, and he was trying to sing too.

But the enemy never came. They just went away. I could see a few of them as they went across the little valley, walking away. I guess they decided that this crazy person wasn't worth taking that day. Whatever it was worth, it was a respected thing, because we walked off that hill alive. Whatever the reason, I feel that my song got me home to see my father.

We are told by our grandfathers and grandmothers that for as long as there are Indians there will be song, and as long as there is song there will be Indians. As long as we sing our songs and someone learns them, there will be new Indian people, for song is our survival tool as a people.

CLIFF SIJOHN is a cultural leader from the Spokane and Coeur d'Alene tribes. His present work is as special projects officer for the Coeur d'Alene Tribal Bingo/Casino. He is a combat veteran of the Vietnam War and was the first Native American to be hired by the Tacoma Police Department. He has made two films, *Circle of Song* and *Spirit of the Wind* (about the special relationship between Indians and the horse); both are about his family and the traditions of the singers and the drummers of the Plateau, which were handed down to him by his father. He was also involved as a writer, producer, and actor in the film *Mee-Yi-Me-Yum* (He Is Going to Tell a Story), which documents Coeur d'Alene tribal stories, and was produced for the state of Idaho through the Lewis and Clark State College.

Jeanette Timentwa. *Photograph by Jill Sabella; courtesy of Washington State Arts Commission*

Native Songs and Seasonal Food-Gathering Traditions

JEANETTE TIMENTWA

Interview and Transcription by

REBECCA CHAMBERLAIN

AN ELDER FROM THE COLVILLE INDIAN RESERVATION, JEANETTE Timentwa lives in the hills outside Malott, Washington. A full-blooded Lake Indian, she was born near Kettle Falls on June 11, 1919. She was married to the late Martin Timentwa and has eight children and many grandchildren. Strong in mind and body, Jeanette is her family's matriarch. She instructs her clan in the discipline and ceremonial gathering of native foods and herbs. They still practice a traditional hunter-gatherer lifestyle that honors the passing of the seasons.

Her home is warmed by a wood stove and is filled with the scent of herbs and teas that she brews daily. In a ceremonial house next to her home she holds winter gatherings, root feasts, and other traditional celebrations. An alcove on the side of her house is filled with dried deer meat, salmon, dried berries, camas, and bitterroot. Medicinal herbs and numerous other foods are constantly renewed. Crates of canned milk, boxes of fruit, and other foods are kept ready to feed large crowds at celebrations. In the yard, several dogs chew on the bones of a deer. Hides hang from trees to dry. A sweatlodge stands not far from the house, and a mineral lake for medicinal bathing is only a few miles away.

Jeanette has acquired several songs, some that have been with her since childhood. As her life progresses through the seasons, so her songs progress through her life. Her primary song permeates her activities. Its force instructs her, makes her work easier, enables her to help people, and assists her in gathering food or finding missing objects. Since an auspicious encounter when she was five, this song has been woven through every aspect of her life, from her initial refusal to accept it to her eventual knowledge of its guidance and protection.

A seasoned survivor of seventy-six years, Jeanette is well grounded in the subtleties of her tradition. Throughout our conversations she made references to aspects of the culture that may be unfamiliar to those not immersed in the traditions. The "winter dance season" is a time when individuals or families sponsor gatherings and celebrate native spirituality. The participants share their individual songs and dances with the support of the community. A "closing dance" is the last dance of the season. Most ceremonial songs are sung exclusively during the winter dance season, then are "put away" or set aside during the rest of the year.

During the dance season, participants often gather in ceremonial houses. Some individuals (such as Jeanette) have these houses built close to their family dwellings. The family or individual that hosts an event feeds and gives gifts to all who have gathered. Beautiful oratories are delivered from the center of the house. In Jeanette's tradition, the "speakers" gather around a specially erected "pole," which symbolically contains the life of the event.

Jeanette, usually reluctant to share personal accounts from her life, made an exception for the sake of this collaboration. Her stated reason for sharing her story now is to inform and instruct the coming generations.

This chapter is based on conversations with Jeanette Timentwa both in her home and during camas-gathering trips in March and April of 1994.

Rebecca Chamberlain

Jeanette Timentwa speaks:

I am a full-blooded Lake Indian. I was raised at Kettle Falls when the salmon were running. I believe in the four seasons. All our tribe believed in the four seasons. Some people have different ways of celebrating, but that is our belief.

I was raised in two different traditions. My grandmother (Katheryn Louie) went to church every Sunday. I could count on one hand the number of times I've been to church; she could count on part of one hand how many times she had missed church. In the winter she would pack my clothes and say, "Now you go to your uncle [Phillip Paul] because he's an Indian doctor. You might learn something. You might be able to help people."

I didn't go to school until I was eight years old—my grandmother didn't want me to. In the spring, we had to go root digging. The first harvest was bitterroot, then Indian potatoes, Indian carrots, wild onion, then the black camas. For everything you have in the supermarket, we have as Indian food.

Celebration of the Seasons

I believe in the four seasons: spring, summer, fall, and winter. I honor each season. Right now I am ending the winter dance season by hosting a closing dance. I'll have my spring root feast in April. There will be names given there. In June, I have a dinner for the salmon and the serviceberries. For my salmon dinner, I bring out all of my Indian food. I'm welcoming the salmon when they get up to Kettle Falls.

My grandmother had a drying rack as big as this house. We would dry the salmon in the summer, then put split cedar between the fish for storage. We had no refrigeration in those days, and the cedar would protect the salmon from insects.

Sometimes we would store the salmon in ice caves. I call them the Indian deep-freeze. We would get a bunch of salmon, put it in sacks, and that was our freezer. We would hang whole deer there, as well. Then we had food for funerals, feasts, dances, or other occasions.

In October, we have what I call the "Indian Thanksgiving." We have a gathering to put away the food. I collect all the food that I've gathered in the summer and put it on the table. Then I put it away until the winter dance season.

I have my spring root feast, I have my salmon feast, I have my Indian Thanksgiving, and I have my winter dances. I belong to the four seasons. That's my belief.

Springtime is my new year. I say, "Why have it in January, when there is nothing going on but cold weather?" But in spring all the flowers, trees, and grasses are growing. The birds and all the animals are having their babies. To me, spring is new year, a new beginning in life.

When I eat a meal, I never eat the last bite. I don't know why, but it's been that way from my ancestors on down. Mad Bear, an Iroquois Indian, explained that. We always feed the earth after we get done eating. You take some food and throw it on the ground. We sprinkle a little food or tobacco or something and thank the earth that lets us be there.

I address each season with a prayer. I say prayers for the berry season in my own Indian way. We pray for everything, like these roots, and the salmon, and the deer. We pray that we will have enough food to last from one season to another. That's my belief, and my children's.

A lot of people are beginning to join me now. They say, "Well, when are you going to have your root feast? We're not going to do anything until you have your root feast." Here lately, I've been having kids out because they don't understand our culture anymore. So I explain what our rituals mean, what our dances mean.

I have my root feast in the spring. That's my new year, as I said. Everything is growing. I'll say a prayer over my roots so that next year I'll have the same amount. In the summer I have my salmon dinner. I say thanks to the Great Spirit that the salmon was able to come up so that I can have food. I serve all the Indian food and say a prayer for that. I thank everybody that comes. I have a little give-away every time that I give a dinner for the seasons. I give away blankets, material, bandannas—whatever I can get, I pass it out.

In October, I have Indian Thanksgiving. I have dried deer meat. I have grouse and all the food that I gathered in the summer. We call it *skoom chum*, which means "the putting away of the food in the fall." We don't bring it out again until the snow comes. Different people have different ways to celebrate the winter season. Me, I have my medicine dances and my give-aways. And I thank the Creator for helping me get through the winter season.

Power Songs

Nobody is ever trained for songs. You find your song as a child. Nowadays, I hear about these people going out trying to find their song. That's not the way it was a long time ago. A long time ago, when you were four or five years old, if they wanted you to find a song, they would take you to the mountains and leave you there. You had to find your way back.

I didn't want a song but it found me. When I was four or five years old, my grandmother had a whole bunch of milk cows. When she finished milking, I would ride one old cow about half a mile out. Then I would jump off and come home.

One day I rode this cow out and didn't come back. I didn't remember anything until I woke up. I had my head on an animal skull. I saw my two uncles, medicine men, standing there.

I looked up and said, "Oh, I must have fallen asleep here."

They both smiled and said, "Oh, she's going to be a coyote when she starts singing."

Then I got up and heard people yelling. My uncle shouted up to the sky and began singing my song. He said, "Now go to your grandmother."

She had a sweathouse built for me. I jumped into the creek, then I went into the sweathouse. I went to sleep in the sweathouse. The next day I woke up and my grandma was building a fire again. I said, "Did I sleep here?" She said, "Yes."

I told her, "I'm hungry." She said, "What do you want to eat?" I said, "Do you have any dried deer bones?" She said, "Yes." So she cooked soup for me, and I ate. Then I went to sleep again.

I forgot all about that experience until I was about forty years old. I dreamed that I had to sing the song. I was ashamed. I said, "I'm not going to sing it."

The next time I dreamed, it said, "I'll break every bone in your body if you don't sing me."

So it happened. I broke every bone in my body. I've got five pins in each leg to this day. My chest was crushed. I was unconscious for twenty-one days. When I came to, a nun and a priest were standing there. I said, "Am I dead?" The priest said, "Almost." I looked around. There were flowers all over my room. There were two men with suits on.

I had been in a terrible accident. I was on my way to be a guest speaker in Trail, British Columbia, at an Alcoholics Anonymous conference. A drunk guy hit me from behind going 100 miles an hour. He rammed my car into a tree and pushed the motor clear through. Both my legs were broken and my chest was crushed. I spent three months in a Canadian hospital and three months in a Brewster hospital.

When I went home the following autumn, my song told me, "You sing me this winter, or I'm going to start in on your kids' bones." After that dream, my daughter came home for Christmas. She said, "I'm going up to midnight mass." I was cooking Christmas dinner, making pies. She said, "I'll be back in two hours and help you cook." Twenty minutes later I got a call. She had stepped out of her car and broken her leg. Still I didn't sing.

Then my son, who works at the Tribal Center, was playing outside and fell down. He got a straight break in his leg. Then I said, "I'd better sing, if it's going to start in on my kids."

I have to be careful when my song tells me to do something. If I don't do it, something may happen to me or my children. My grandson broke his leg. My granddaughter ran out of the house, ran to the bridge, and got a straight break in her wrist. This time it was because I didn't give away everything that my song had told me to.

I must do whatever it tells me. The animal tells me what to do. That's why I'm getting ready now. It will help me; I have that much faith in it.

Before I sang my song, I used to drink. Every time I heard my song, I would go out and get drunk. I finally sang it, and I've been singing it for thirty-two years now. I sing it in the wintertime at the dance. I sing it when I go root digging. It tells me I will never go hungry. My song is with me all the time—I don't have to put it away.

I believe in my song. If I didn't sing it, I wouldn't be alive today. It has been with me my whole life, protecting me all the time. It protected me all the years I was drinking. It helps me with everything I need. Somehow, somewhere, I will get the money for what I need. Things will work out. But being me, I worry.

I tell the people when I'm singing, "When you go hunting, if you want to sing my song, go ahead and sing it." So they do—I give permission to anybody who comes to my winter dance. If they want to sing it when they're out digging roots or out getting food, they can go ahead and sing it. Singing my song makes work a lot easier. You have to believe in what you're doing in order to succeed.

One thing my song is good for is helping if you have a drinking problem. If you stand by the ceremonial pole and I sing my song, then you'll never drink again. One man staggered up to my pole one night and said, "Hey, I need help." That was the first time I sang to help anyone. I said, "Well, I'll try." He's been sober twenty-three years.

My uncle, who was a medicine doctor, sang this song of mine until I was eighteen. He died when I was in my early twenties. He said, "Now I haven't got much longer to live. When this song comes to you and tells you what to do, you do it or it will punish you." I really didn't believe him.

I'm not an Indian doctor like my uncle. An Indian doctor knows what problem you have. He even knows what you are thinking about. My uncle knew that someday I would be singing. He knew what kind of animal I had. When I disappeared as a child, he knew where I was. He was very powerful. He would say, "That person is coming. They will be here before sundown or before midnight." Things like that. He also knew who was going to die.

I also get the feeling before someone is going to die. I know someone will die, but I don't know who. I told my kids that my uncle probably knew I was too ornery and mean. He probably didn't want me to know who was going to die.

All the animals have a song. That's how we get our songs, you know. I have two songs. The deer song is a food song. When I have my dance, I surround the house with another song. It's a song that protects my house and the people in it—the old bull snake song. I found it when I was about six or seven years old. I used to tease bull snakes. I was teasing one in my grandma's barn. I'd chase it and it would go one way, then the other way. Finally, I guess it got tired of me. I looked inside the barn door to see where it went. It blew something into my nose and I passed out. When I came to, my grandma was putting water on my head with a cloth.

She said, "What happened?"

I said, "I don't know. I was chasing that bull snake."

Oh, she gave me heck. "You had no business teasing it. It's more deadly than a rattlesnake if it gets mad."

A few years later, the bull snake told me that it would protect my house and everything I had. I didn't have to sing its song.

My deer song doesn't allow itself to be recorded. At ceremonies, when someone else's is recorded, and I start singing, even if their song is taped, my song never records. I don't know why—it never works. The song seems to stop the tape recorder.

Five or six students from the University of Washington attended one of my ceremonies. I told them, "No taping. No picture taking. This is something sacred to us Indians." I can always tell where there's a tape recorder. Before I sang, I hit the floor with my cane and their tape recorder popped open. All their tapes were unwound. I said, "I told you—no taping."

You'll have to come to one of my dances so that you can hear my song. But I won't allow a tape recorder there.

[Jeanette makes references to both coyote and deer in discussions about her song. She also mentions a bull snake song. Because it is forbidden to reveal specific information about the source of one's guardian song, she is deliberately vague about which animal influences her primary song. The "deadly" nature of the bull snake mentioned here is symbolic rather than literal. Although a bull snake can kill a rattlesnake, the bull snake itself is not poisonous. Also called gopher snakes, they feed primarily on gophers.]

The Deer Woman

I don't particularly like to be called "Deer Woman," but a lot of people call me that. I always wear this beaded deer medallion, you know. This medallion is my protection. My animal isn't really on this medallion, it just resembles it. It's a deer, but not what I have on my medallion.

I dreamed about a deer. I can't eat deer from August or September until the following spring when my winter dance is over. When I put it in my mouth, it tastes like blood.

If you dream of something bad, you try to prevent it. You try to do whatever the dream tells you to do to prevent it. If you have a good dream, you thank your dream and hope it comes true. People don't talk about their dreams very often. It's something sacred to us Indians, to know what our animal wants us to do. I have dreams and visions I'm not allowed to share.

One time I was having my dance. My grandson and I came out the back door, and there was a deer standing near the venison drying racks. My grandson said, "That deer wants to get on the drying racks, doesn't it?"

It looked at us. We came inside and it was still standing there. We didn't want to tell the other people. It ran up the hill a ways and kept looking at us. Then it went into the brush, and we never saw it again. We had enough, so we didn't kill that deer.

I tell my grandson that when he hunts a deer, be sure to thank the deer when it falls down. It's laying down its life for our food. Be sure to thank the deer, that's all I ask.

Some people misuse a deer. They kill it and just take the hindquarters. They have a hard time finding any deer.

Deer have always protected me. One time, I was picking huckleberries at Stampede Pass and I saw a little fawn eating huckleberries. I talked to her and I kept picking.

All of a sudden I had a funny feeling, and I looked behind me. There stood a big black bear. I didn't know what to do, so I picked up my big five-gallon bucket and walked toward the deer. All at once, the little doe put her ears back and ran right past that bear, and she kicked that bear right in the mouth. That bear went down, then it ran as fast as it could over the hill. Then the little doe came back just wagging her ears—a fawn, a yearling.

I told my friend, "That little deer kicked that big bear in the mouth and that bear took off running." Deer can really be that mean. I don't know what that bear would have done if she hadn't done that.

Another time, I drove my granddaughter to Yakima to get settled at Kinman Business College. On the way back, about three o'clock in the morning, I just couldn't drive any more. I said, "I'm going to sleep right here. I'm just twenty minutes from home, but I still might have a wreck." I turned off the road and went to sleep.

All at once I heard somebody singing. I had a pickup and there were deer all around the truck. There were about forty or fifty of them. Then I thought, there must be a reason they woke me up.

So I started the car, turned on the lights, and went home. I got home and my cousin, who's a medicine man, was sitting up. He said, "What woke you up?" I told him, "Well, you know what woke me up—the deer."

He said, "I just heard on the radio about a shooting not far up the road, right where you were. There was a shooting and some of the guys took off on foot. Maybe that's why the deer woke you up. Those guys might have kidnapped you to get your pickup."

I told him, "That was probably the reason."

Finding Food

When I can't find my Indian food, I sing my song. Then I happen to wander into my food accidentally. When I first started to sing, I was told what to do and how to prepare my food. I was told everything I served had to be Indian food. No other kind of food was allowed. I was told, "This has to be done. That has to be done." I was told that I had to have twenty-two servers. I thought, how am I going to get all that Indian food? But I got it.

I gathered all Indian foods, from the bitterroot to the yellow bell. Tiger lily is an Indian food. Wild onion, mushrooms, Indian carrots, Indian potato, camas, cous, Indian celery, the salmon, deer, eel—all are Indian foods. Easter lily is an Indian food. So are serviceberries, huckleberries, and chokecherries for jam. There are many more.

Up in the Methow Valley are bitterroot, tiger lily, yellow bell, and Indian carrots. Now we can't get to our foods, thanks to the progress of the white man. There are "No Trespassing" signs in all those places. We used to be able to gather our bitterroot at Twin Lakes, and now we can't.

Finding the Song

If someone in my family finds a song, they can sing it. You can feel it when they are singing. You can feel their power by the pole. If you don't feel or see anything, you know they didn't find that song. It's probably somebody else's song, but they just want to be singing themselves.

The spirits sometimes take care of you so that no harm comes to you. Some people hear songs in nature. The spirits like some people and protect them. Some they don't—it all depends.

The spirit of the land is still here. But some people are trying to destroy this world. Look at the earthquakes—that was predicted by some old Indian doctors. I think animals in this world must be getting mad because everything they depend on is being destroyed. Things are going to happen. Some people are going to have a rude awakening.

Children must be taught some things, but I think children should be left alone if they are singing. If they find a song, they can follow through on it. If you try to teach them, I think that's wrong. I don't tell my kids to go sing this song—they would just be pretending. If a child is more grown up and hears a song, I say, "Keep singing, it's probably yours anyway." We don't teach these songs: your animal spirit has to tell you.

To my people, you have to find a song when you're very young before you can really say, "This is my animal" or "This is my spirit." Some people look for it when they are old. To me, that's looking for something that's not really meant for you. Sure, the spirit will talk to you and all that, but if an animal finds you, then you have more power.

Our chief used to sing a salmon song, but I never really tried to learn it. If he passed it on, it probably went to someone in his family. Each person has his or her own song.

Our people catch salmon at Chief Joseph Dam now, though the fish are not nearly as plentiful as they once were. My grandson used to fish there and have big catches. But he was one of the gifted ones. He started fishing when he was eleven. He could catch fifteen or twenty when others caught none. He could go out hunting where you wouldn't expect to find deer, and he'd get deer.

He had some powerful experiences at Chief Joseph Dam. He used to camp out and fish at night. In the morning I would bring him breakfast and he would give me the salmon he got.

One time I got there, oh, about six in the morning. He was fishing and only had three or four. I said, "What's the matter, slow night?"

He said, "No, I had a weird thing happen last night. I was sleeping and all of a sudden, I heard a song. This little old lady was standing by me, singing this song. She told me not to fish until daylight, that way I would catch more."

Then he started singing it to me.

I said, "Oh, you'd better listen to your dreams or whatever happened. Maybe you were even awake."

He said, "I was supposed to get a cigarette from you, take one or two puffs and throw it in the river." So we did that. I wasn't there but an hour and he caught nine big salmon. I told him, "Gee, that's enough. We should go home."

So I took him home. He quit fishing at night. Instead he would come down early in the morning and fish. Then he really started catching a lot. Many people wouldn't catch any while he was there.

So I don't know—I guess he must have had a song.

[Jeanette's grandson Robert, referred to here, was killed in an automobile accident. Another grandson, Leo, continues to hunt for her family.]

JEANETTE TIMENTWA, an elder from the Colville Indian Reservation, continues to instruct her clan in ceremonial gathering of native foods and herbs, guided by songs.

REBECCA CHAMBERLAIN, a Northwest writer, storyteller, and educator, holds an M.A. in English literature from the University of Washington. Her work includes fifteen years of collecting and preserving Northwest Salish (Lushootseed) language, stories, and cultural traditions. She has taught courses in storytelling, literature, and oral narrative for Lesley College, Seattle Pacific University, and Western Washington University. She currently teaches at The Evergreen State College.

Native Songs
Taught by Ellen W. Saluskin
(Hoptonix Sawyalilx)

VIRGINIA R. BEAVERT-MARTIN

ELLEN SALUSKIN (1890–1993) WAS A WIFE, MOTHER, GRAND-mother, horse-woman, shaman, gathering guide, community leader, and singer. Her life of 103 years was dramatic in both its simplicity and its breadth of experience. Her story reflects the lives of many of her contemporaries and demonstrates her unique gifts, which she generously shared with her people. This article serves two purposes: to introduce the phenomenal woman who was my mother, and to illustrate the lifestyle, beliefs, and traditions of my people through her example. The story of her life links the old generations with the new to show how the Yakima culture has survived.

The Early Years

Ellen Saluskin (Hoptonix Sawyalilx) was born in 1890 at Sih (now known as Zillah), on the Yakima Indian Reservation. She lived on the reservation her entire life. Because the Bureau of Indian Affairs could not spell it correctly, her name became Hoptonix Sawyalilx. Business associates called her Hoptonix, but the elders and her family referred to her as "Ilaan" or "Ellen."

Ellen's parents were Oscar Wantux and Timinsh (Emma) Sawyalilx. Oscar was a Palouse Indian enrolled as a Yakima. He graduated from Carlisle Indian College in

Ellen W. Saluskin (Hoptonix Sawyalil<u>x</u>) and daughter Virginia.
Courtesy of Yakama Nation Museum

Pennsylvania and returned to Yakima country where he fell in love with Timinsh, the daughter of Yakima George and X̱aẖish Sawyalilẖ. The Wantuẖ family did not practice traditional ways; they were Christian. So, Oscar took Timinsh to Spalding, Idaho, near Lapwai, where they were married in 1889 in the First Presbyterian Church by the founder of that church, the Reverend Spalding. [Authenticated by Mylie Lawyer, historian from Lapwai, Idaho.] One year later, Ellen was baptized as Baby Wantuẖ at that same church. Oscar died when Ellen was still an infant. Her maternal grandparents took her in, changed her name to Xapt'iniks Sawyali'lẖ, and raised her in Sih until she was married at the age of thirteen. She was named Ellen Oscar when a government nurse tried to enroll her at the Fort Simcoe Indian School—where she was turned away because she had tuberculosis.

Ellen's people were descended from the "old" Chief Wiyawict through his son Twaynat. All of her people were shamans. X̱aẖish Sawyalilẖ, a Klickitat Indian, was a well-known herbalist doctor and a spiritualist exorcist who cured Ellen of her tuberculosis with herbs and mud baths.

Except for the Christian Wantuẖes, Ellen's people all practiced the Longhouse Waashat religion. Worshipping is done through dance, following the teachings of the prophet who arose after death at Sih. He eulogized the Creator and prophesied the natural divine revelations, predicting the future of the Native people. These revelations are interpreted in the *waashat* songs that are still sung today, having been passed down orally through the leaders of the Longhouse, including Ellen. Other worship songs, brought back by different prophets, have similar messages, and these are shared by the Sahaptin-speaking people. These songs are not composed.

The Sahaptin people cherish the longhouse belief. They believe that we are all equal within nature. We are creatures of this earth and therefore we are all related. This is one song drummers sing at the Sunday *waashat*:

> *Anakuu isinwiyaa, chinki tiichamki, aa, aa, aa . . .*
> When He spoke the Word about this world . . .
> *Kuumaan ataa, iwanwi-shaamsh timaash, aa, aa, aa . . .*
> Ever since that time, the message has been coming down from
> Above to earth.

Besides religious songs there are social songs. The Sahaptin tribes held an annual social dance to celebrate *Papa-waaw-shtay-mat*, the Engagement Dance. Held in the longhouses each summer, it was accompanied by drumming and singing similar to the Sunday worship *waashat* ceremony, but with differences easily distinguished by the elders. The dance was held for the young men and women who had come of age, to show that they were eligible for marriage. This was during the time when the Sahaptin families practiced arranged marriages, a custom which reinforced the traditions, culture, and linguistic stability within their clans, and was usually done for sound economic advantages as well.

The ceremony began when a young woman was taken out on the dance floor by the female elder of the family. They danced from one end of the floor to the other, with arms linked, until a young man with his male elder went out to meet them. The young man placed his left hand on the left shoulder of the young woman, and they danced forward and backward a few times. If the female chaperone approved, she did nothing. If she disapproved, she pushed the hand off, reversed the girl, and danced away with her. When a couple was approved, the medicine man, acting as the priest, came out and placed his staff on top of the boy's hand; the drummers raised their hand drums into the air and the men *waykw'ansha* (cheered). This announced that the couple was officially engaged.

My mother smiled secretly as she related her own story:

It was exciting to watch them lined up abreast; the men in the east and the women in the west side, dancing to the wonderful sound of drumming and singing. The girls were beautiful in their brand new taffeta and velvet wing dresses, wearing bright-colored necklaces and large white shell earrings. The boys were handsome in their blanket chaps and bright-colored shirts, their long hair strips decorated with colorful beads hanging down around their faces. It was truly an exciting time for everyone.

Ellen's cousin, who was three years older, was very mischievous. She talked Ellen into dancing out on the floor without parental consent—Ellen said she thought they were practicing. When Harris Wataslayma put his hand on her shoulder and it was not pushed away, they became engaged. A few weeks later, Harris's grandfather came to talk to Ellen's family. Despite her grandfather's argument against this early marriage, the family decided to follow tradition to preserve their culture, since both families were equal in status. Ellen's great-great-grandfathers on both sides were warriors, and they participated in the Indian War when Major Haller was defeated at Toppenish Creek in 1855. Harris's great-grandfather, Elit Palmer, was a chief. His name is recorded on the Treaty of 1855 with the U.S. government. His maternal grandfather, Shishaash (Porcupine), was a shaman.

As was customary, both prominent Sahaptin families had set aside dowries for the eldest child. Harris's mother had collected *ina-waa-wiksh*, a male dowry, but she died before she could witness his marriage. An aunt supervised the dowry exchange.

Horses, cattle, porcupine-quill decorated buckskin costumes; headdresses made of furs and eagle feathers; rawhide parfleches filled with dried deer meat and fish; other parfleches filled with Canadian woolen blankets and beaded buckskin wraps; and Salish goat-hair robes were exchanged for the *tmay-yiksh*, female dowry, put away by Ellen's mother and grandmother for her. Beaded bags, beaded dresses of buckskin and tradecloth, cedar baskets, wampum and shell beads, five-gallon corn-husk bags filled with dried roots, nuts, and berries were her offerings. Ellen recalled that her wedding veil was made of dentalium shells, the cap had six rows of shells across and hung down to her waist. She said there were gold coins attached to the veil hanging down over her face. These material things were exchanged at Harris's and Ellen's *Pápshxwiit*, Indian wedding trade.

Ellen and Harris were taken to Tap'ashnak'it (Edge-of-the-timber), the village located on Bickleton Ridge, to live with his maternal aunt for three years. There Ellen was tutored in the Columbia River dialect and culture. Then they were brought back to Ellen's village to live. He too, had to learn a strange culture and language. Harris never attended school, and Ellen was refused admission because of tuberculosis. Instead, both were taught by their home communities in the traditions of their people. Both Harris and Ellen became shamans.

They were celibate for those early years because they were so young. Later, they had three children: Oscar, 1916, deceased; an infant daughter who died in 1919; and a daughter (me) born in 1921. When the government was forcing the Indians to accept allotments, they could not spell my father's Indian name—Wataslayma. He was issued an English name—Harris (Henry) Beavert. [The Dawes Act of 1887, commonly known as the Allotment Act, required that reservations be divided and each tribal member allotted a parcel. The remaining land was claimed by the U.S. government and made available to Euro-American settlers.]

Ellen said Harris was a good provider and a kind man. He farmed their land and found employment with local farmers. They might have been uneducated but they were both shamans and socially equal in the Sahaptin culture. In 1926, she divorced him when he became addicted to alcohol. Four years later he joined the Shaker Church, quit drinking alcohol, and became the minister of the Satus Shaker Church, where he served until he succumbed to heart disease in 1990.

A Healer and Teacher

Ellen continued to live in Sih and practiced shamanism until she married Alexander Saluskin, a Salish-Wenatchee Indian, in 1928. Alexander was raised by his grandmother at Leavenworth, Washington. His mother, Chashtkw'i Timentwa, was married to a Yakima Indian named George Saluskin. Alexander was brought to Fort Simcoe Indian School, where he received his education and was later enrolled with the Yakima tribe. Ellen and Alex had one son named Rudolph Valentino Saluskin.

Alexander was active in tribal politics, and was the chairman of the Yakima Nation for many years. After he retired from this post, he was employed by the Washington State Parks as an archivist at the Fort Simcoe Park in White Swan. There he met Dr. Bruce Rigsby, an anthropologist-linguist, who came from the University of New Mexico. Together they developed an orthography with a practical linguistic writing system. This was the first time the Yakima-Sahaptin language was written down with proper sounds recorded. Ellen and other elders insisted that the proper Sahaptin-Yakima name is *Iiyaakii'ma*—that is, Yakima, not Yakama.

The dictionary, used by several Sahaptin tribes today—including the Yakimas—was not completed until 1975. By then, Dr. Rigsby had returned from Australia, and I had graduated from Central Washington University with a degree in anthropology to fulfill a promise to complete Alex's work on the dictionary.

Ellen too had promised Alexander, when he was terminally ill, to encourage the children to continue to learn and practice their Indian culture and not to mourn his death. She purchased a motor home and took them on the powwow trail. Because they were talented dancers and bead workers, they won many prizes at powwows during their travels. Ellen was the singer and drummer when they did group dances. Many of the songs and dances that they performed were loaned from other tribes, but had come to Ellen through family ties.

Ellen's marriage to Alexander had temporarily disrupted her practice of shamanism, because Alex was Catholic and he did not approve. After he died in 1976, however, she resumed the practice to protect the children in her family. Ellen held a strong faith in the Longhouse religion that was passed on by her family, and she became a leader of the Longhouse.

The food songs are part of the Longhouse Waashat religion. Ellen was a leader of the women at the "old" longhouse at Toppenish. She led them when they went after the wild food plants for the annual Ceremonial Root Feast. She taught the women food songs, fasting practices during food gathering, and the prayers the diggers recite to the Creator to preserve their sacrosanct relationship to the creations: Mother Earth, the water, plants, wildlife, and to the human spirit. Ellen emphasized, "The food gatherers must revere this holy connection to the food through prayers. They must purify their mind and body. When this food is partaken by those who are physically and mentally afflicted, it becomes a healing medicine to their spirit and body."

Ellen Saluskin, third from left, with son Rudy, taking part in a root festival
prior to digging bitterroots for the Toppenish Creek longhouse, ca. 1949.
Courtesy of North Central Washington Museum, Grace C. Gardner Collection

Ellen followed the traditional belief in creation. It advocates the equality of all living things and emphasizes the responsibility humans have to protect them. Many songs carry this message.

Respect for sacred foods is also conveyed in song. When a man shoots a deer or a boy catches his first salmon, he thanks it for its life and calls it "*pyap*, older brother." When a young girl plucks a berry for the first time or is initiated into root digging, she thanks it for its life and calls it "*pat*, older sister." There are appropriate songs for this ceremony for all initiates. This creates a bond with the divine creation.

When Ellen felt well enough on Sundays, she asked me to cook wild foods for Sunday breakfast at home. We invited her grandchildren and great-grandchildren. They came dressed up in their Sunday clothes—wing dresses, buckskin vests and ribbon-shirts—to "eat breakfast with grandma Ellen." She was teaching them the proper way to set the holy food on the table and two food songs. She told the children: "Water was created for all of us. Everything depends on water for its life, without water we cannot live." They learned that the natural foods are healthy. She told the children: "If I didn't eat *pyaxi* (bitterroots) and *sikawya* (breadroots), I would not have lived to one hundred years old." The children really miss their grandma and her Indian breakfast.

She taught the children stories and songs about wildlife and how to interpret them in dance. Many of the songs and dances were given to us by other tribes, having come to Ellen through family ties. William Shelton, who carved canoes and totem poles and lived at Tulalip, was a shaman from the Snohomish tribe. He adopted me and my brother Oscar, and he taught my brother two shaman songs. His daughter, Harriet Shelton Dover, taught me the dances she performed at the Winter Dance to these songs. Ellen learned them too. Her mother-in-law, Louise Saluskin, taught Ellen the song for the Swan Dance, a Salish legend about the Swans at Lake Chelan. A Canadian man named Dan McJoe taught us the song for the Thunderbird Dance. My uncle John's wife, Ida Wynookie, taught my mother the song for the Cougar Dance. She was the daughter of Tommy Thompson, chief of the Celilo band from Oregon. Ellen, in turn, shared her family's song for the Farewell Dance, the Legend-About-Beacon-Rock, about a legendary landmark at the Columbia Gorge, written down in the Yakima Indian Legend Book, *Anaku Iwacha*.

Ellen was talented in other ways as well. Although she never attended a formal school, and could not read or write English, she was a prudent manager of her personal and financial affairs, negotiated her own land leases, and kept a personal bank account. Ellen learned, as a little girl helping her grandfather, to be a horse trainer. She once owned a stable of Kentucky thoroughbred horses, which she trained and

raced. Some old-timer track men remember how she doctored their horses with Indian herbs at the race tracks. Ellen drove trucks during the wheat and pea harvests
and worked in the canneries during World War II, which earned her her Social Security. Ellen was a seamstress too, and she designed many beautiful Indian teepees.

One special talent that Ellen had, though rarely used, was to sing a reunion
song to bring families together again after one of the spouses had abandoned them
for another. She did this by means of song and telepathy. They went to the highest
mountain, where Ellen sang songs lamenting all of the grief and sadness experienced
by the one left behind. This was transmitted to the "wanderer's" subconscious during
his sleep and he became restless and began worrying about his family. After several
sleepless nights, he began to find fault with his new love and he returned to his family. She helped both men and women in this way. Thanks to her, there are couples still
living happily together, their children all grown up.

Grandma Ellen taught us a lullaby we would like to share with you. The infants
love it. The baby is rocked in rhythm with the song, which is repeated over and over
until the baby falls asleep.

> *Maask, maask, yaa, yaa . . .*
> Starlight above . . .
> *axaa taamli-kaasam, aatay, aatay, paaxi . . .*
> shower baby with your shimmering light . . .
> in the eyes to sleep in peace . . .

We are thankful to Hoptonix Sawyalilx for her wisdom and the songs she shared with
us. We shall never forget them. Her spirit will be felt as we sing and dance.

VIRGINIA BEAVERT-MARTIN, a full-blooded Yakima Indian, was raised by
her great-great-grandmother who taught her the traditions of her people, including
two dialects of Sahaptin: Klickitat and Yakima. She is also conversant in the Umatilla
and Warm Springs dialects. She participated in the production of the *Yakima Indian
Language Practical Dictionary* (Johnson and O'Malley Consortium, 1975), and *The
Way It Was: Anaku Iwacha: Yakima Legends* (Franklin Press, 1974). Ms. Beavert received a Federal Fellowship to research history at the Smithsonian Federal Archives
in Washington, D.C. She currently teaches Sahaptin at the Heritage College in Top-

penish, where she works with young American Indians to preserve the Sahaptin language, songs, dances, legends, and poetry. She has been selected by the Washington State Arts Commission as a participant in the Master/Apprenticeship Program, to teach the Sahaptin songs and dances learned from her mother.

Song Traditions of the Yakama

BRYCENE A. NEAMAN

"When I listen to these songs I crave for more"

WRITING ABOUT OUR TRADITIONAL SONGS IS A NEW EXPERIENCE for me. This is not the way the Yakama have taught our songs through the years. We have no song books with written words and music for people to sing along and learn our traditions. The beauty of our culture is that one learns from listening and taking songs into one's heart. We hope that the readers of this book will share that experience, by listening to the music the way that we do.

I see this book and recording as a great beginning to educate the mainstream population and correct stereotypes. It is a book that will help restore the pride of being Indian. When I listen to these songs, I crave for more. I hope that new listeners will feel the same way.

In my efforts to help non-Indians gain a better understanding of our music, I first stress the importance of the singer's feelings. We do not analyze or interpret our songs, for their importance comes from the experience of the singer. The Yakama sing from the heart. Sometimes the chant and song create a purely spiritual feeling, and there is no translation or interpretation. The total experience, not merely the meaning of the lyrics, is meant to inspire the soul.

In many instances, we strive to keep the songs in their original contexts. Tribal members recognize the obligation to maintain our traditions the way they were intended by our ancestors. Because of this concern with preserving tradition, bringing our songs to the public has not been easy. We want the songs to be treated with respect, honor, and dignity—as our teachers have always done.

The ways of teaching and sharing songs are unforgettable processes in themselves. I reflect on how our songs have been shared by my cousins, friends, and ancestors. Every time I learn a song I think of how it came to me, and then I think of all those to whom I will teach the song. This sharing process is natural to our people and is an inexorable part of the song tradition.

Sharing of Songs

From time immemorial, songs have been shared within the tribe and at such intertribal gatherings as powwows and trade meetings. Today, the Yakama people also have new composers of traditional songs. Two such contemporary composers are Fred Hill, Sr. and the late Leroy B. Selam. In true Northwest Plateau Indian fashion, these men have shared their songs with me, and they are fine examples of contemporary, yet traditional, song bearers. They are highly regarded singers in our region.

The Selam family is one of a group of well-respected traditional singers on our 1.4-million-acre reservation in south-central Washington State. Elder statesman Howard Selam and his brother, James, are faithful keepers of traditional knowledge in the Yakama country and have shared songs, family history, and ways of life with the community. James has taught many people about Yakama songs, including the historically significant work songs inspired by life on the Columbia River. Two such songs that connect us with the river are the Willow Song and the Feather Dance Song.

James has taken an active part in passing on our traditional ways. Because of his words, many younger Yakama eyes now see in a more traditional manner. He has helped impart traditional values and wisdom such as respect of elders, respect of nature, the pursuit of spiritual guidance, and knowledge and pride in being an Indian. James's son, William, exemplifies the middle-aged generation who have chosen to preserve the traditional ways of the family and tribe. Many of our people call upon the Selam family to help in traditional activities.

The Meninick family is another of a group of well-regarded traditional singers in Yakama country. Johnson Meninick, a program manager for our tribal cultural resource program, is a top-notch traditional war dance drummer. Johnson has traveled throughout the United States and Canada sharing the "old" war dance songs from our region. He has formed a group called the "Yakama." Johnson, who once served as

The Selam family, Northwest Folklife Festival, 1992.
Photograph by Lou Corbett; courtesy of Northwest Folklife

The George family, Northwest Folklife Festival, 1992.
Photography by Lou Corbett; courtesy of Northwest Folklife

our tribal chairman in the 1970s, has knowledge of traditional beliefs that make him a valuable cultural resource.

It would seem odd for me not to mention a group of young cousins who are called "Indian Nation." This group of brothers come from a well-respected traditional family that originated on the Columbia River. "Indian Nation" is primarily made up of the Totus family. Near the east-central edge of our reservation is a community called Satus. Two very influential brothers helped the Satus community obtain a new building in 1955 called the Satus Longhouse. They were Burt and Watson Totus, who were also my grandfather's cousins (my grandfather being Isaac Johnson Albert, 1901–86). Such men have rekindled a strong religious feeling in our little area. I should also mention Gilbert Onepennee, who once told me, "This is your longhouse; don't be afraid to come in when you can." There was always a closeness to these older men, who are now all deceased but have left many of our younger Yakamas with a strong traditional religious foundation. The unique drumming sound of the "Indian Nation" drummers is a legacy of this strong traditional heritage.

The George family is another notable bearer of Yakama song tradition. The late Leander George was a scholar and master of songs for this family. He and his wife, Delores, have taught their children family songs, ceremonies, and customs in the Yakama manner. The family has a large repertoire of modern and traditional songs. The modern compositions are based on traditional models. The family has also won many song and drum competitions. They carry on Leander's legacy.

Many Songs, Many Purposes

It is through such teachings that our people keep in contact with our Creator. Our sense of connection involves remembering that the self is one with the earth, the spirit, the Creator. When we feel this connection between earth and our hearts, we often express it in song. "Having a song in one's heart" means to rejoice, to remember, and to bring solitude to our souls. Songs are one of the essential needs of our being in its quest to remember the relationship with Mother Earth. Being in harmony with nature is celebrated through song—the earliest way of communicating. This spirit is the recognition of our being one with the First People.

This relationship between song and nature is demonstrated through our traditional views of plants on the Yakama reservation. The tribes and bands would often come together to sing about the upcoming season of gathering roots and berries. We sang and still sing today. Many traditionalists would rather not release these sacred songs pertaining to berry gathering; working with non-Indian programming in regard to music makes me support our traditionalists' concerns.

Songs have been used for centuries—in our belief, from time immemorial—for social ceremonies and gatherings. The special songs composed to honor men and their feats may be heard today. The chant of warriors returning from battle is still part of our tribe's tradition. Today, the chants of modern-day warriors—veterans and other men and women of valor—are sung by the Yakama Warrior's Association. Another example of an honoring ceremony is Elder's Day, which has become a significant annual event on the tribal calendar and has been incorporated by our tribal students.

Remembering Who We Are

The lifestyle of the Yakamas has changed greatly since the years following the Treaty of 1855. On June 9 of that year, near present-day Walla Walla, Washington, the Yakama Nation of Indians and the United States met to negotiate and sign the treaty, which gave the name "Yakama" to the fourteen bands and tribes that have come to constitute the Yakama Nation. (Yakama, Palouse, Pisquose, Wenatchapam, Klickitat, Klinquit, Kow-was-say-ee, Li-ay-was, Skinpah, Wish-ham, Shyiks, Oche-chotes, Kah-milt-pah, and Se-ap-chat). The treaty also reduced our territory by almost 90 percent—from 10.8 million acres to 1.4 million.

Fortunately, memories of this event and many subsequent incidents have been collected from elders in interviews and oral histories, giving us a deeper understanding of our people. In many ways, Yakama Indians have come to lead lives very similar to those of mainstream Americans. We deal with similar problems in family, work, and the political arena. However, there are differences that constantly remind me that we are not part of the mainstream culture. My involvement in education and in the "Spirit of the First People" project comes from a desire to expand people's understanding of both differences and similarities.

By teaching others about our songs, we hope to help people better understand a culture and history not always accurately reported and described by members of other cultures. Some of our songs, and our language itself, were discouraged in the early 1900s. In American history the "melting pot" attitude prevailed. "Melt away the Indian" was the philosophy, and this was a true injustice to our people. So the proposal to share our songs, language, and customs makes us hesitant—justifiably, in my opinion. Some Indian people have asked me, "Why *now* does the American

Yakima dancers, Fourth of July Celebration, 1893.

Photograph by J. Hamacher; courtesy of Cheney Cowles Museum, neg. L84.494.66

society want to know?" I answer that they probably do not want to know, but when we are given a chance maybe we can reach and educate their children to know that our ways are important. We plant the seed in these next generations, and things might be better for our children as well.

Many historians have written cruel justifications for settlers moving into our area by calling our land and its people "uncivilized," a term used to describe many people who did not participate in the overwhelmingly dominant culture. This term has bothered me. To our people, "civilized" means to be in harmony with nature, to live a life close to the earth. It means to be able to communicate with a spirit greater than ourselves. This spirit exists in song; and to an Indian person, being in touch with the spirit within song means being in touch with the spirit within one's self. I remember the songs that were taught to me by members of my tribe and others. I sing a song sometimes to remember who I am and what makes me unique.

The chieftains of our tribes have truly been challenged to preserve our right to live in peace and harmony with nature. I believe that Indians have an irrevocable right to their spiritual relationship with nature. It has been the basis of our culture that nature and the land are close to our hearts. Our ancestors have given us wise teachings, and they are the way of our future.

I hope that the day of reckoning has passed—but if not, that we will again be ready for the challenge facing our indigenous lifestyle. Despite the years during which our traditions were outlawed, and the challenges that the modern media present for us, we still keep many of our traditions alive. "Spirit of the First People" is both evidence of that continuing life and a tool to help us keep these traditions strong.

Our people can only benefit, I believe, from the increased understanding that sharing our heritage can bring. If there is no attempt at communication, it is our children who will suffer. My hope in contributing to this project is that we can bring together my Washington coastal brothers and sisters along with the Salish and my Plateau people in contributing a lesson for all people.

My work and living on the Yakama reservation provide me with insight into my commitment to such education and to the destruction of negative stereotypes. We have been fortunate to have a museum on our reservation that addresses these stereotypes. This is a place for people to understand what a significant contribution Indian people have given the United States. The museum was built in part from the dream of Nipo Strongheart (ca. 1891–1966). Nipo, an avid collector, accumulated over 10,000 books and artifacts, and willed his collection to the Yakama Indian Nation upon his death. The museum, which was completed June 9, 1980, in many ways fulfilled Strongheart's dream of educating non-Indians as well as Indians about "our" story.

My hope is as Strongheart's was in a dream recorded in the Yakama Indian Nation oral history:

Pipe Prayer

Great Mighty Maker, a needy one stands before you. I am He! Warm my heart and guide my words that they shall speak only which is not false. Open the hearts of the listening ones, that the words which you shall give me may enter therein and dwell for all times; that we might walk together as brothers, and know one another with an understanding heart. So, the time when you shall call us, we may come before you with no blood on our hands.

> *Prayer given me in the dream of the night,*
> *Monday morning at 2:00, January 22, 1945*
> —Nipo Strongheart, Yakama Nation

BRYCENE NEAMAN was the master of ceremonies at the Spirit of the First People concert at the Folklife Festival in 1992. He is a Native drummer/singer, storyteller, and author enrolled with the Yakama tribe. He presently works at the Yakama Indian Nation Youth Treatment Center. He was the curator at the Yakama Nation Cultural Heritage Museum in Toppenish from 1988–95, and has been a commissioner with the Washington State Arts Commission and the Washington Centennial Commission, and has served as a board member of the University of Washington's Burke Museum.

Makah Music

Preserving the Traditions

LINDA J. GOODMAN

AND HELMA SWAN

THE SPIRIT OF THE FIRST PEOPLE HAS SURVIVED OVER THE centuries largely as a result of the determined efforts of the elders, who have generously shared their accumulated knowledge with the younger generation. It takes a great deal of energy and hard work to keep a culture's values, beliefs, music, and ceremonies alive. If even one generation fails to teach the next, the tribal heritage suffers greatly. Thus the very survival of a culture depends on its methods of passing this knowledge on to its children. Surprisingly, these methods are seldom examined.[1]

The Makah Tribe of Neah Bay, Washington, on the northwestern tip of the Olympic Peninsula, has created some interesting and enjoyable ways of educating its young people in traditional music and culture. Like other aspects of native life, these methods of teaching have evolved over the years to adapt to changing cultural circumstances. Helma Swan,[2] a Makah elder and herself an outstanding singer, is today perhaps the foremost authority on Makah practices for conveying musical and cultural traditions. She was exceptionally well educated in these traditions as a child, and maintains a vast store of cultural information which she has been teaching to others for many years. This article is based on discussions over a period of years in

Note: This article is adapted from Goodman and Swan's book, *Singing the Songs of My Ancestors: The Makah Life and Music of Helma Swan* (University of Oklahoma Press, 1999).

Helma Swan, Northwest Folklife Festival, 1992.
Photograph by Lou Corbett; courtesy of Northwest Folklife

which she described old and new Makah musical teaching methods, along with their strengths and weaknesses. Helma has been greatly concerned about the continuation of the "spirit" of her family and tribe; her hope is that this work will contribute to the preservation of the Makah traditions.

The Place of Music in Makah Life

Traditional songs and music have a very special place in the life of the tribe. In earlier times the most important function of Makah music was in ceremonies meant to uphold the power and position of the chiefs. Music was also critical in the correct performance of rites of passage (ceremonies connected with birth, puberty, marriage, and death), secret society activities, medicine and curing, hunting, fishing, whaling, warfare, games, and recreation (Densmore 1939; Curtis 1916; Drucker 1951; Ernst 1952; Goodman 1977, 1991; Sapir 1913; Sapir and Swadesh 1955; Sproat 1868; Swan 1870). Some of these activities still continue, and appropriate music is performed for them; in other instances, the activities and associated music have disappeared.

In the past, most Makah songs were personally owned pieces of property, and some were considered more important than others. A set of rules, handed down orally from generation to generation, guided the tribe in the proper handling of the songs. Included were such topics as who could own songs, how they were to be passed to descendants, who would perform them, when and where they could be performed, how they were to be taught, who could learn them, and who could loan them or give them away. The chiefs, who were traditionally the most politically powerful men in the tribe, owned the most important songs, which supported the Makah social structure (Goodman 1978:83–88; 1991:223).

A system of hereditary ranking formerly determined Makah social organization. Three classes of people existed: chiefs and their noble families; commoners—those distantly related to the chiefs (not in the direct line of descent); and slaves—those captured from other tribes in warfare. Chiefs and their families had rights of ownership to specific songs, dances, masks, costumes, and ceremonies (Drucker 1951:243–48). Ownership and use of these items enhanced their status, prestige, and wealth. Commoners, who in the order of ranking were considered less important people, owned fewer objects and owned songs that did not have much status and prestige. Slaves had no social standing whatsoever, and owned no songs (Goodman 1986:380–81; 1992:24–28).

The Makah ceremonial system essentially supported and reinforced the social structure. Great feasts, potlatches, and a variety of secret society ceremonies could be hosted only by chiefs and their families. Members of the other classes usually attended and participated in some of the activities, which often involved fairly large numbers of people (Drucker 1951:366–410). Songs of the chiefs were sung on these occasions and strengthened the social standing of the owners and their families. However, there were several avenues by which commoners could acquire a certain amount of status and prestige. For instance, particular individuals could develop special skills and become outstanding hunters, whalers, or medicine men or women. Specific music was also essential for the proper performance of these activities, and the related ceremonies were often (though not always) done in private or with only a few people present (Goodman 1974: Field Notes, Tapes, Transcripts of Interviews 1974–94; 1992:28).

Today, there are fewer occasions for the performance of Makah music and fewer types of songs are performed. Feasts and potlatches continue as major ceremonies and are still hosted by individual families who are descendants of the former chiefs. Secret society ceremonies and curing ceremonies disappeared long ago, as did most of their associated music. Songs to accompany bone games and other recreational activities still exist, but most songs connected with hunting, fishing, whaling, and warfare have faded from memory. In days past, many of the men and a few of the women went alone into the woods to seek a guardian spirit who would guide them throughout their lives and give them individual power songs as well. These songs, and the accompanying personal religious activities, are no longer performed.

The potlatch, now called a "party" or a "potlatch party,"[3] is considered by the Makah to be their most important remaining ceremony. Formerly hosted by a chief for the purpose of displaying his inherited privileges and increasing his power and prestige, the potlatch ceremony is now performed by the descendants of the old chiefs in order to honor an important person, to display family-owned privileges (including songs and dances), or occasionally to transfer hereditary rights in the appropriate manner (Goodman 1991:224). Potlatch parties are now held on the occasion of a birth, naming, girl's puberty ceremony, birthday, marriage, wedding anniversary, or a memorial honoring a deceased person one year after his or her death.

A contemporary Makah potlatch begins with a great feast and includes the singing of appropriate Dinner Songs. At the conclusion of the meal, the serious portion of the ceremony begins. One after the other, members of each family who wish to participate stand, sing, and dance several of their treasured family-owned songs, and immediately give away gifts and money as payment to the audience for witnessing this performance of their inherited privileges. This activity continues and includes families from each of the visiting tribes in attendance, as well as the Makah.

Finally, many hours later, members of the host family sing and dance a number of their songs. This is followed by the giving away of great quantities of gifts and money, along with announcements presenting the people being honored, names or songs being given, and so forth. The entire "party" often lasts from eight to twelve hours and offers an opportunity for many families to participate in the singing and the dancing, thus reaffirming their place in the society and strengthening and renewing tribal traditions.

It is clear that music has always been an essential element in the proper functioning of Makah society. Songs have helped support and maintain the social order, have fostered economic survival, and have strengthened the physical health and the mental and religious well-being of individuals, as well as of the tribe as a whole. Therefore, the proper "passing on" of the musical heritage has been of utmost importance to the Makah people.

Old Makah Ways of Teaching Music

Since tape recorders and other recording devices did not exist before the late nineteenth century, and since the Makah themselves had no system for writing down their music, it had to be passed on orally. Knowledgeable individuals talked about and sang the music so others could hear and learn it—a method of transmission called the "oral tradition." This was the primary manner of teaching Makah music.

Family-Owned Songs and Dances

In the past, the musical training of young people was far more rigorous than it is today. Each family had the sole responsibility for teaching its songs and dances to family members in order to perpetuate its musical traditions. One learned in one's immediate family setting, and did not know exactly how or what other families were taught. Helma Swan,[4] the oldest surviving sibling of a family of thirteen, received her musical training from her father, Charlie Swan. Much of his adult life revolved around singing and dancing Makah songs and upholding the family traditions at potlatches. Since he owned the Swan family songs, which were inherited from several chiefs, he was responsible for their perpetuation; therefore, during the 1920s and 1930s, he taught and drilled his children. When an occasion arose that required the dancing of family-owned songs, his children were ready. Helma Swan recalled some of her father's teaching methods:

If my dad was going to teach us a new song he would make us sit down and listen to it 'til we were very tired of it! He'd just play the drum and sing it, every day—every day. I've never known but just a very few times that he didn't sit down and sing. He would have to be sick, not to sing a little bit. . . .

It seemed like from the time I was little, I had to listen to my dad [sing], whether I wanted to or not. I guess because the boys were so much younger than me he really didn't try to get them all that interested. The younger [boy] did take interest for a little while, then later he didn't care much. You had to be interested in order to do something like that. Actually, when I started out I wasn't that interested either. My dad would say, "Now sit down and listen because you have to know these songs sometime in the future. Maybe you'll wish you had listened to them. . . . So he'd sing and I would listen. Sometimes he would sing this one [song] and I really used to listen to it because I thought it was just beautiful!

Every day he'd sing a different song—three, four, five of them, maybe even a dozen in a day—and he'd make me sit and listen. He wanted the rest of the children to listen, but they'd say, "We've heard those songs too many times, we don't want to listen," and away they'd go. But I would have to sit there and listen. . . . He'd always say, "This [song] belongs to so-and-so." And then he'd sing another song. "Well, this belongs to so-and-so." And he'd say, "You'd better listen to these songs, dear, because one of these days, people are going to ask you to help them. Or somebody's going to ask you what their song sounded like, and you're going to have to help them. And that's what I'd like you to do— is to help them." Then I used to sit there and think, "What is he saying that to me for, be-cause he knows I can't do that. He knows I can't sing!" And I'd get kind of resentful inside. I didn't ever think I'd learn how to sing.

Aside from listening to and learning the family's songs, the children had to learn to dance them as well:

My dad used to make us practice dancing almost any time—in the evening if he was home, and if he felt like it on Saturday or Sunday—then we'd all have to dance. He'd start singing and he'd say, "Okay, girls, get out there and let me watch you dance." We'd run around and get our blankets or shawls—anything we could get ahold of—and put them on. We weren't particular as long as we had something over us.

So he would start in, and my mother would go about her cooking while he'd watch us to see if we were doing okay, and it wasn't any special time, but he just kept us going like that all the time, so this way we couldn't forget. . . . We didn't mind it at all, we just got used to it, I guess. . . . If he didn't like the way we were stepping or the way it looked, he'd go over the song again. Just where the extra beats come in, he'd say, "All right, it's com-ing—when you say such-and-such [a word]." . . . We couldn't quit until we did it just the way he wanted us to dance.

Costumes were an essential part of any song and dance performance, and each child was responsible for his or her own:

The only time we got particular about [the costumes] was when it was [potlatch] party time; then we'd race around and look for them. My dad made us all make our own costumes. I think this is the way that he made us appreciate what we had. And believe me, we took care of them. We were sort of proud of them, you know, because we accomplished something [by making them].

Importance of the Family Masks

Certain songs and dances required the use of particular masks, which also were owned by the family who owned the accompanying music. There were spirits in the masks, and they had to be treated properly. Helma's father often said that the masks had to know and be familiar with all the members of the family who would either dance with them, or sing and dance, while they were being used in a ceremony. Helma recalls:

My dad made a wooden box—it was kind of big . . . it must have been about three feet by four feet, with a handle on it so it could be a suitcase . . . and it always sat in the hallway near my brother Emil's bedroom. The masks were in there, and my dad fit all the whistles in there that went with the masks. The button blanket fit on the top, too, to keep everything from rattling around. The whistles were on one side and the masks were on the other. He lined the box on the bottom side where the masks were, so they wouldn't break. They all just fit in there perfect so there'd be no rattling and no busting anything. . . . My dad always kept the box upright, so the masks would face the north.

My younger brother, Emil, never went [with us] to the [potlatch] parties. Most of the time he stayed home, alone. One night when we were all away from the house, all of a sudden he heard a noise—like you're clicking your teeth. He got up and looked around, went into my mom's room, didn't find anything, so he went back to his room, laid down again and thought nothing more about it. Pretty soon he heard it again. So he stayed in the kitchen. . . . He started drinking tea—he was kind of a tea bug. He heard it again, so he looked over real slow, and then he knew where the sound was coming from.

And then he went back to his bedroom and stayed there. And when he closed his door he heard it again, but this time he heard the whistles blowing, too. And he never said anything for a while, he just kept quiet—never told Mom or Dad anything—until the second time it happened. Then he finally told my mom.

My mom told my dad, so my dad sat us all at the table, and he sat my brother Emil there, too, and he said, "Now those things [masks and whistles] don't know you, that's why they're making a lot of noise like that. . . . You're the oldest boy, and you're supposed to be the one to take after me—do the things that I'm doing now, and take my place, because I don't have too long," my father said. "I don't know whether I'll be gone today, tomorrow—you never know. You should be the one to take over what I'm doing in this line of Indian dancing, Indian tradition. You're the oldest boy; you're supposed to be learning all these things, but you never listen to me. This is why this is happening to you—these things don't know you any more. Instead of *you* doing it," Dad said, "*She's* doing it. Do you ever hear *her* telling me that she's hearing those masks the way they're carrying on? And the whistles? She doesn't say anything because she's used them—she's familiar with them and they're familiar with her. And they don't know *you* because *you* aren't trying to walk in my footsteps!" He explained it to the rest of the younger children, who told him, "Well, that never happened to us!" Dad said, "Well, you children are learning to dance. The masks are familiar with you because you have danced background for the masks and have been dancing with them constantly, where Emil has never stepped foot in there. Neither has the oldest daughter!"

So nobody said anything about it any more. About a year or two later . . . my oldest sister was home all by herself, and she didn't know that any of this had happened to my brother. And then she heard the same thing. . . . She got scared . . . [because] she heard the whistles blowing plus she heard the chatter of the teeth. And she ran out of there! Later my dad told her the same thing that he told Emil. Then he said, "You shouldn't have run out of there . . . because these things will take your shadow away from you." This means that your life isn't going to be very long. My brother and my sister didn't live very long. They died, both of them, several years later.

Neither one of them would do what Dad told them. He said, "You better start doing something so those things will familiarize themselves with you." And they just wouldn't do it. It made him real unhappy, but there was nothing much he could do.

Thus there were definite consequences when one ignored Makah cultural teachings and did not participate in the musical life of the tribe.

Women's and Men's Dance Routines

Makah and other Westcoast (Nootka) women, some of whom had excellent reputations as singers and dancers, also taught the music and dance traditions to the children. They worked with the girls, teaching them "background" or "side dancing," which was the normal female dance routine. Helma Swan recalled several people who helped her learn to dance when she was young: "[My dad's aunt] Annie used to teach us—she and Francis Frank's wife Effie Frank. And Effie's mother and dad. The four of them used to teach me to dance. And my cousin Francis Frank was there, too,

Children rehearsing the Paddle Dance (a group dance), August 16, 1984, in preparation for a Makah Day performance. *Photograph by Linda J. Goodman*

Boys practicing the War Dance, August 16, 1984. This group dance is performed
for entertainment on Makah Day, an annual celebration in late August at Neah Bay.
Photograph by Linda J. Goodman

of course, and he would watch what we were doing. . . . They always start you off [learning] background."

In order to perform "background" dancing, the women moved into a large semicircle or U shape, located behind the lead male dancer(s), and then executed a number of subtle arm and foot movements in unison with their fellow dancers. This created a lovely flow of movement, beautiful to behold and an effective complement to the roles of the male dancers.

The males danced in a counterclockwise circuit in the central portion of the dance area, using specific movements and steps related to the particular characters they were portraying (usually animals or other supernatural creatures). Often it was the older men who taught the young men to dance: "How did my dad learn to dance those Wolf Dances? Well, his cousin Francis Frank had watched these all his life, so Francis taught him how to dance them. And then Michael Brown [another family member] taught my dad the Hamatsa Dance."

The "lead dancer" roles were typically reserved for men, but occasionally a woman might dance a lead role if there were no males in her family available to do so: "It wasn't really allowed for a woman to dance the Wolf Dance . . . but my dad didn't have any boys [to dance for him], so I learned, and that's why [two times] I got to do the Wolf."

Teaching a New Chief

Charlie Swan's aunt, Annie Williams, from the Clayoquot tribe on the west coast of Vancouver Island, also taught him some of her father's songs, which she later gave to him at a potlatch she hosted in 1930. Songs were ordinarily transferred from father to the oldest son, but sometimes this pattern could not be followed. If a chief did not have a son, someone else had to receive his songs, dances, masks, and costumes. Often they would be given to the oldest living daughter, who would be their caretaker until she could pass them on to her son, grandson, nephew, or another carefully selected male relative whom she deemed worthy of this honor.

Annie Williams received the belongings of her father, Benjamin Cedakanim, a chief among the Clayoquots, who had no sons. Since Annie had no children of her own, she selected her nephew, Charlie Swan, to inherit her father's chiefship and to receive these chiefly goods, which included many songs, dances, masks, and a family curtain. (A family curtain is a very large canvas cloth with painted crest designs that tell the family history. It is hung inside the community hall when there is a potlatch hosted by the family.)

Charlie had to be taught the songs and dances before he could use them, and Helma Swan recalled that Annie was instrumental in accomplishing this: "Annie came to Neah Bay and worked with my dad to teach him the songs she was giving him. She came a number of times and stayed for about three months each time and she taught him the songs. She stayed in our house and she taught him every night."

Another form of musical education was necessary for young men who were to become chiefs. Individually each had to attend what has been called "Indian school," where he learned how to be a chief and was taught all the musical knowledge essential to his position. The specific details of this type of education are no longer known, but Helma Swan was present for some of her father's education that took place in the village of Clayoquot in Canada in 1930:

My dad had to go to school every day. Every morning at eight o'clock he and the chiefs would all go to this one longhouse that Francis Frank had, and they'd sit in there. And they'd either start talking to him, or they'd start singing. And my dad would just have to listen . . . like he made me do. And different ones [Canadian chiefs] would teach him things to do, what to say. And there were times that the chiefs had song sessions—enough just to break the tension of teaching him what to do. . . . And they would sing [a song] over and over 'til he learned it. So this is how he learned. . . .

And Captain Jack [one of the Canadian chiefs] stayed with us. He stayed at Annie's house for a week [to teach my dad] and then he'd go back [home]. . . . Then he'd come back to Clayoquot again to teach my dad some more.

Learning a Song Received as a Gift

Sometimes a chief would give a song as a gift to a person from another tribe. Such a gift would be given only to someone in a chief's family, and there was a proper procedure for teaching the new song:

This is what they used to do a long time ago when my dad got his songs. . . . He had to invite the Canadians over here and . . . keep them under his roof. And every night while they're here he's under obligation to call all the heads of the Makah tribe, and the singers and the drummers, and have them over to his house every night for a week . . . so they all could learn the songs. . . . Our family would feed all the visitors every day, three times a day. Sometimes one of my dad's relatives would say, "We'll get together at my house tonight, we'll sing at my house," and this would take a little of the pressure off my dad for a night or two. . . .

When my dad was doing this, it is what we call, *ha há wakt sub*, which means something like, "eating at the feet of a special person." I have to invite two people from our tribe, who aren't chiefs, and they come and eat with the visitors and all the rest of us. The visitor tells why he came—what he is here for—while everyone is eating. Then it is up to the people who are not chiefs to spread the news to the rest of the tribe. They are the witnesses . . . to tell the people what happened here. Then the tribe knows that we have been given these songs and that our visitors are here teaching them to us.

The new songs are actually presented by the old owner to the new owner at a large potlatch which is hosted by the former owner for this particular purpose. An announcement is made concerning the transfer of song ownership, and then the songs are sung. Afterward, the audience is paid to remember that this transfer took place, and later, when they return home, they are to tell others about this event, so it will not be forgotten.

"Singing Sessions"

A somewhat different kind of musical learning experience was the "Singing Session," where people gathered at one of the homes in the village and spent the evening singing the songs of those in attendance and telling stories. This was one of the primary methods of maintaining a strong Makah singing tradition. Held in an informal setting, such pleasurable activity continually renewed the songs in the minds of the adults, while offering the children an enjoyable learning experience:

They did a lot of those singing sessions, *badá.patl,* in the old days. This is the reason they remembered songs and never ever forgot. They were doing it all the time, and when they felt like they wanted to, they'd get together and sing—just plain sing! They never seemed to get tired of singing. And that's when the kids had to come, and they sat and they kept still. You never did see a child running around!

These were always at night, because the men were working in the daytime, or fishing. After dinner the people would start coming in—like six-thirty or seven o'clock. . . . They'd sit around and sing and then maybe tell old Indian stories in between singing. Then they'd say, "Well, let's stop and sing again." And they'd start in singing again. Then maybe somebody else would pipe up and say, "Let's learn mine, too, while we're at it." This is what they did, so it wouldn't be dull.

We used to do this once or twice a week, sometimes three times. My dad did this at our house ever since I can remember, from the time I was a little child. If everybody stayed late, they'd serve something to eat about nine-thirty or ten o'clock. It wasn't anything elaborate. . . . They had these nice big crackers, and they'd give you crackers and butter and tea or coffee. If they wanted to go all out, they'd make Indian dumplings . . . or fried bread or buckskin bread . . . all depending on how the cook felt. So this was our entertainment, then.

About the time of World War II they stopped having the singing sessions. Everybody just quit. One of the main reasons was because we had what they call blackouts. Then everybody was quiet. Everybody was afraid, a little bit . . . that the Russians or the Japanese would land. So our windows were all blocked up and everybody was made to stay home. . . . Then after that time, there were no more of those singing sessions.

As Helma Swan notes, the singing sessions were one of the casualties of the war, but in addition, many other parts of the musical and cultural life were also beginning to change.

Newer Makah Ways of Teaching Music

Although much has changed since the time of World War II, a thriving Makah musical tradition continues. The children are still being taught, although not in all the ways formerly described. The oral tradition, with some changes, remains the primary method used.

As previously stated, when Helma Swan was a child, her father used to sing the same songs over and over, day after day, and the children had to listen and learn. Today's children have tape recorders and often their elders will record songs for them to listen to whenever and wherever they wish. This should be an ideal situation for learning. However, since no one is forcing the children to sit and listen repeatedly, they do not do it regularly, nor with the same attention and concentration as required by parents and grandparents in former times. If they try to sing or dance to the tape or an occasional videotape made for the same purpose, often no one is present to correct their errors and help them improve. Thus the children become familiar with a variety of Makah songs on their tapes, but they have not internalized them as fully as in days past.

Family Teaching Methods

Elders still spend time personally teaching their children and grandchildren, but the method is somewhat different. For example, Helma Swan has created her own teaching technique. She makes her children and other relatives ask her questions; then she feels free to give them the necessary information:

I remember how I used to be kind of bitter about how my dad used to do. . . . He'd make us sit down and he'd tell us [things]. I'd think to myself, "Well, why should I sit and listen to all that stuff. I already listened to it before." And then maybe I had too many things on my mind at that time and I didn't want to listen.

So, I sort of had to learn to talk to my children in a roundabout way—make them ask about a few things—and then I'd start telling them. Otherwise, if I didn't do that, I know they'd feel like I did. So I made up my mind, "I'm just going to make them ask me a question." And I'd carry on the conversation to where they'd have to ask the question. Then I'd sit down and say, "Well, do you have anything to do? Do you have to go anywhere?" Then by their answer I'd know, and they'd have to sit down and listen. . . .

[On Makah Day] when my daughter and I come home for our rest or something, or lunch or coffee, then we'll sit down. I feel like I don't want to sit down and approach her unless she asks me a question. She often brings it up herself—"How or why did so-and-so do this or do that? I thought they weren't supposed to do it at that time." And then I'll start telling her that they did it this way or that way, and then we get our general conversation going.

Even though this question-and-answer format is Helma's chosen method for teaching family members, the musical and cultural education of each of her three children was slightly different because of the specific circumstances surrounding the upbringing of each child:

With my oldest boy . . . we lived with my mom and dad off and on [when he was little], so I imagine my son must have learned a lot from my mother and dad. He just listened as a little kid, to the way my dad talked to us and told us how to be and how not to be. . . . My dad taught him in that way. Now, I don't question my oldest son in any way because he always talks just like my dad used to talk. . . . I guess he must have listened and learned. When I think it's time for us to sit down and talk, we sit down and talk, but I've had more chances to talk to the younger boy than to the older one.

The youngest one hasn't been going to too many potlatch parties, so I've had to sit him down more than either of the other two children and talk to him. He has a habit of asking me questions. He doesn't go right into anything; he sits and asks about it and then thinks about it. Sometimes I'd practice singing when he was sleeping . . . and he'd hear me. He's heard me sing a lot more, I guess, maybe because I never learned to sing when I had the other kids. I wasn't singing at all when they were little.

The summer of 1973 was the first time I sat my daughter down and told her what she should tell her children. Because she was younger than my oldest son, and I don't think she'd sat down and listened too much to my dad . . . so I've had to talk to her and tape some of the songs for her. But she knows the songs, I have to give her credit for that. She knows the songs because she'd say, "Tape this for me. Tape that for me." I had tapes for her . . . so she could teach her kids.

No one in Neah Bay currently teaches the music and dance as Charlie Swan or the chiefs' wives used to do in the past. However, in the early 1970s, when Helma began teaching her husband his songs and dances (previously he had not been interested in learning them), she used many of the same techniques her father had used with her in years past. She knew many of her husband's family songs quite well, having heard them performed frequently at the numerous potlatches she attended as a child. Therefore, she was able to help him learn them many years later:

When I first started teaching Wimpy, I had to begin by singing the song the way my dad used to do. He'd say, "Now, sit and listen! You're not dancing, you're going to sit and listen to this song until you're tired of it! Then you'll know just exactly where the beat comes in, where it changes." So that's the way my dad taught us how to dance, and that's the way I taught Wimpy. . . .

I said, "You can't talk Indian, but you'll hear one certain word, and when you begin to recognize that word, then . . . you'll know that your steps are going to get different, and then from that point on, you count how many steps, because there aren't that many beats in there for it to be that hard." I told him, "Count how many steps you're going to take. It may be one, two, three, or [it may be] one, two, three, four, and then it will go back again to the same beat." So this was how he learned.

Although Helma applied a number of the old-style teaching techniques used by her father, she also employed the newer method of using tapes and cassette recorders. She did not sing the song over and over as her father would have done; rather, she recorded it and let her husband listen to the tape numerous times while he learned the song. However, she did work carefully with him when she taught him the proper dance steps and body movements. These he had to do over and over again while she watched and corrected him.

Learning to Sing as an Adult

Charlie Swan never taught any of his children to sing their family songs. He made them listen and learn to dance, but none of them ever actually tried to sing the songs with him. According to Helma, "None of us kids ever sang Indian songs; my dad didn't ask us to. But he knew we were learning them because we had to sit and listen. Every single day!"

For unknown reasons, apparently no other families in Neah Bay taught their young people to sing, either. None of today's elders ever learned to sing as children or teenagers. After they became adults, some of them had a strong desire to continue the musical traditions, and therefore—by imitation, memory, and sheer determination—they taught themselves to sing. Helma Swan was one of these people:

> I was able to do that dance as long as my father could sing it for me. . . . But then when he died, in '58, I didn't know how to sing it. . . . I had to learn all by myself—just thinking about it. And I realized then that I knew the song, but I never did try to sing it before. But I just made up my mind that I had to do it.

Helma also had to begin singing in public, and she started by singing one of her husband's songs at a potlatch party in 1971 or 1972, held in the village of Queets (located farther south on the Olympic Peninsula, approximately 90 miles south of Neah Bay). Since she had never sung Indian songs in public before, and had not been trained to do so by any of her elders, she was quite nervous when she began:

> One day they had a party there [at Queets] and we were there. So the Makahs started to sing, after the party got going. And Wimpy (my husband at that time) said, "I wish I could get them to sing my grandpa's song." I said, "We could try."
> [Not too long before this] we had gotten a reel-to-reel tape from one of the Makah women, and my husband's grandfather's song was on it. And I [had] sat there and started learning that song all over again. I hadn't heard it for years. So I played it over and over every time after my husband went to work, and I learned it. It didn't take me too long, 'cause it just automatically came back.
> So, at that party at Queets as the evening wore on, all the Makah singers were feeling sick and they said they couldn't sing Wimpy's grandfather's song. . . . By that time my heart was just *beating*—it was just *pounding* . . . even in my ears! That's an awful feeling! "All right . . . I'm going to try anyway!" I said. I borrowed a drum . . . and went over to the Canadians who were there and I asked, "Could you folks help me sing? I'm going to sing Jim Hunter's song." . . . So I have five of them helping. . . . Even if all of them weren't singing, I felt like I had moral support. And I started singing. . . . And all the Makahs who were there—they stood up. They were standing there for a while watching me, and their mouths were open—because I was singing! They never heard me sing before, but I guess I did all right. . . .
> After that, I started going to most of the parties again, and eventually these songs all came back. When you hear some of them, your memory keeps working on them for a while and then that brings you to another one. And then you're thinking of that one and eventually you think of another one. Because I have heard them all my life. But . . . there's some that don't ever come back.

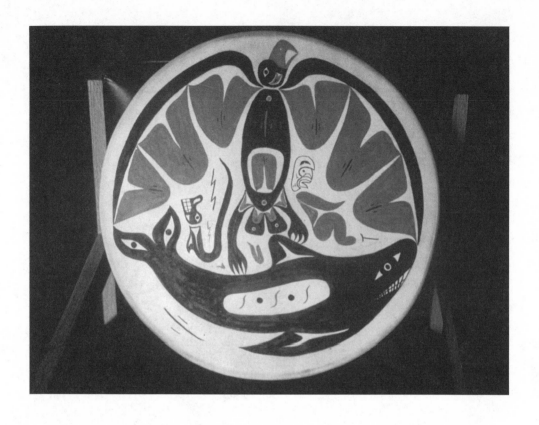

Makah drum with painted Thunderbird, Whale, Sea Serpent, and human characters.
Created in 1988 by Makah artist Roy Smith, Neah Bay. *Photograph by Linda J. Goodman*

Once Helma got back some of her husband Wimpy's family songs and had learned to sing a number of the Swan family songs, she had to continue to practice them so she would not forget them.

I would practice all by myself. That's the way the old people used to do a long time ago. I remember when I was about six, seven, or eight, I used to hear Mrs. Annie Long Tom singing—first thing in the morning, real early. She'd be alone, nobody with her, and she'd be singing up a storm! All the time. And then my dad sang alone—every day. Except when he wasn't feeling good. We'd know that he wasn't feeling good then, when he didn't sing.

So I practiced alone, too. I would just take the drum, sit down, and sing. I would be alone in the house. My husband was working and my youngest son was in school. So when they were gone I could sing.

Practicing for a Performance—a "Warm-up"

Today, when it is time for a family to host a potlatch party, they are not immediately ready to perform, since the children are no longer exposed continually to the music and dance as they were in the past. After the family gathers and decides which songs they will sing, and in what order, they begin practicing them periodically at someone's house. These practices may occur about once a week for several weeks before a party, or sometimes a practice may be held only once, about a week before the actual event. If a potlatch (or occasionally some other type of public performance) is not imminent, there are no practices.

A "Warm-up" party is the final musical preparation for a contemporary potlatch party. A Warm-up usually is held by the host family during the week preceding the potlatch:

A Warm-up party is where you get together and sing through your songs. Each one who's coming [to the potlatch] sings his or her songs. You'll start with number 1, 2, 3, 4, 5, and everybody will sing. We each start our own songs, but then everybody joins in and sings. By the time we're through, we know who's going to sing at the [potlatch] party and in what order.

Warm-ups are a *lot* different than the song sessions we used to have, because you only spend *one evening* there. You don't spend two or three evenings a week. A Warm-up is only just before the party. . . . The family that's going to have the party hosts the Warm-up and decides on the time and the place. They pay for the meal at the Warm-up, too. So this is all they do now to prepare [the songs and dances]. It really isn't enough. They don't know the songs that well now like they used to, and things don't always go as smooth as they did in the past. But the parties still do happen, and we still have singing and dancing for them.

Makah Culture Classes

A newer method of teaching songs and dances has developed over the past thirty years or so. This approach is based on a Euro-American educational model of teaching music in the classroom. In the mid-to-late 1960s, elder Nora Barker (who died in 1979) began teaching Makah language and storytelling as part of Makah culture classes in the Neah Bay public schools. Later she was joined by a series of other elders. Ethel Claplanhoo assisted Nora in this work for a few years, as did Helen Peterson occasionally. Sisters Isabel Ides and Ruth Claplanhoo taught Makah basket weaving for a short time. For a brief period in the late 1970s, several Makah men—elders Hugh Smith, Roger Colfax, and Ham Green (all deceased), and John Hottowe—sang songs and told stories to the children in the Makah culture classes. In the late 1970s and early 1980s and for a number of years following, elders Helma Swan and Hildred Ides, from Neah Bay, and John Thomas, from Nitinat, teamed up to teach the Makah language to the children in this program. The two women also told stories and taught the children Group Dance songs and dances. (Group Dance songs are entertainment songs that may be performed by anyone in the tribe. Most are no longer family owned. These dances are performed for Makah Day; for public non-Makah celebrations; and sometimes at potlatch parties [Goodman 1991:226–27].)

The program has continued to develop and improve, and the children now study Makah language, customs, art, music, and dance on a weekly basis. Helma Swan and several younger Makah women continue to teach Group Dances to the children:

Maria [Pascua] and I do the singing and drumming. Cory [Buttram] and Yvonne [Burkett] get the kids lined up and then teach them the dance. They correct them if they are not stepping right or not doing the movements in the right way. It takes all four of us to teach those kids. There's a lot of them and it's hard work.

The kids in school today learn several dances—they learn what we call "The Four Part"—this is a Canoe song that was created by Young Doctor long ago, and it has four parts to the dance. First the kids do the "paddling-in" part, where they paddle into the center [of the dance area]. Next they are in a line and dance the part where their paddles go up in the air and to the sides and backwards and forwards. For the third part, the kids face each other and they hold their paddles with both hands [horizontally in front of them] as they sway from side to side in time to the music. For the last part, the kids paddle back to shore. So this is the four-part dance which we teach them. Then they learn several other Canoe songs too.

We also teach them what we call the Makah War Dance[5] (which is not at all like a Plains Indian War Dance), a Spear Dance, a Knife Dance, a Sea Serpent Dance, a Fan Dance, and some others. . . . We are now teaching the kids to sing these songs, too. So now they can sing all of these songs and also dance them.

Only the Group Dance songs are taught in public school. Family dances are still taught at home, privately by each family.

Rehearsing for Makah Day

Makah Day is a festive event which celebrates Makah life and culture every year during the third weekend of August:

. . . The reason we celebrate Makah Day now is because the government in 1926 set us free and our people decided, well, we're going to have Makah Day now. Before this, the government had forbidden us to have bone games or Indian dances. I don't really know why the government didn't want us to Indian dance. They were strict at that time. . . . That was why the Makahs went to Tatoosh Island to do all this. But, after 1926, we could bone game and have our Indian dances right on the reservation. So then Makah Day was started to celebrate our freedom.

Once the government changed its policy, the Makah could bring their celebrations back onto the mainland, instead of holding them on an offshore island as they had done for approximately forty years before this. As one might expect, Makah songs and dances are an important part of the Makah Day celebration. Group Dances are performed by younger children in the morning and by teenagers and young adults in the evening.

About a month and a half before Makah Day, a practice schedule is set up. Each year in July, the children and young people begin coming to the community hall to practice once or twice a week for two hours at a time. A group composed of a few elders and a few young and middle-aged adults does the drumming and sings the songs. Usually several younger women work with the children, teaching them the dance steps and movements. The singers also watch and add their comments concerning dance movements and corrections they feel should be made. Makah Day rehearsals continue in this manner for about four to six weeks. As the practices near their end, each child must also have an appropriate red, black, and white costume, which is usually made by a family member.

On the appointed day, the younger children, dressed in their costumes and ready to dance, arrive at a specified time and place. The dance instructors have them move to the blocked-off street in front of the Senior Citizens' Center, where the singers are awaiting their arrival. Then they begin the performance, which ordinarily lasts about an hour. A similar type of performance, but with additional dances, is presented in the evening by the teenagers and young adults in the school gymnasium. Good performances are appreciated by all; the children enjoy participating, and know they are helping to preserve and perpetuate Makah traditions. Often, after they have grown up, they look back on these years and these performances with a great deal of pride.

Hope for the Future: A Young Male Singing Group

Over the past five years or so, a number of young Makah men in their twenties, thirties, and early forties, have become interested in learning the music and continuing the traditions. They have therefore been taking an active role in learning traditional Makah songs and performing them at potlatch parties. Since most of these young men did not grow up with continuous teaching from either parents or grandparents, and since no one sang the songs to them day after day, they have not had the specific learning advantages that were available to earlier generations. However, they are serious, dedicated, and are working hard to learn to sing properly. Some of their family elders are now instructing them, sometimes they learn from tapes, and at times Helma Swan works with them when extra rehearsing is needed before special potlatch parties. She tries to teach them the nuances and subtleties that make the music uniquely Makah.

The young men in this group essentially are in training to become knowledgeable singers and future song leaders who will carry on the tribe's musical traditions. (In 1994 the core group consisted of Greig Arnold, Spencer McCarty, Harry "Champ" McCarty, Jr., Andy Pascua, Micah Vogel, and Brian Parker. Others who participated from time to time included Joe McGimpsey, Ted Noel, Steve Jimmicum, Thomas Parker, Michael McCarty, and Greg Colfax.) They are learning the songs of each family when requested to do so, and then they sing the proper songs for these individual families when asked to perform them at potlatch parties. The group has a good, solid vocal sound, and members are gradually improving their "Makah musical sound." Several of the younger Makah women occasionally sing for their families as well; however, such singing has traditionally been a male task, and people generally feel that the men should still be responsible for most of it.

Helma Swan teaching musical subtleties to young male singers at rehearsal
for the Oliver Ward memorial potlatch party, Neah Bay, September 9, 1994.
Photograph by Linda J. Goodman

Although many changes have occurred in Makah life and musical teaching techniques since Helma Swan was a child in the 1920s, still a number of the musical traditions remain strong. The musical "spirit" of these First People runs deep and will continue to survive because the Makah are determined to sustain and maintain this essential part of their lives.

Notes

1. Although James G. Swan, the first schoolteacher in Neah Bay and an early researcher on Makah culture, spoke in general of Makah culture and described some of the ceremonies, he never talked about musical teaching methods (1870). Other authors discussed specific ceremonies but omitted information on the musical transmission process (Colson 1953; Curtis 1916; Densmore 1939; Drucker 1951; Ernst 1952; Sapir 1911; Sapir and Swadesh 1939, 1955; Sproat 1868). Only Helen Roberts (who prepared Edward Sapir's 1910–14 field notes for publication) briefly mentioned musical teaching methods. She stated that each "high-born family" had at least one master singer who was carefully chosen and trained. The training period was difficult and involved much prayer, fasting, and memorizing. Someone in the family who was already a master singer was responsible for training the young ones (Roberts and Swadesh 1955:202–3). This is essentially all the information that exists concerning Makah or Westcoast (Nootka) musical training.

2. Helma Swan's grandmother became a good friend of James G. Swan and later took his name as a gesture of esteem. There are no biological ties between the two families.

3. Potlatches and other ceremonies were outlawed by the U.S. government in the late 1880s (Annual Report of the Commissioner of Indian Affairs 1890:224). Since the government did allow the Makah to have parties, however, tribal members began to use the term "party" whenever they were intending to hold a potlatch. The tribe has continued to use the term "party" even though the ban on potlatches was lifted in the 1930s.

4. All quotations in this chapter are by Helma Swan and relate to her knowledge of Swan family musical education methods, unless otherwise noted. Interviews were held periodically between 1974 and 1994.

5. The Makah War Dance includes no buckskin costumes or Plains Indian feathered war bonnets. The men wear a cedar bark headband with eagle feathers stuck in and standing straight up, around the perimeter. They carry a bow in one hand and arrows in the other and dance single file in a line which moves counterclockwise around the dance area. The women dance single file behind the men. All do a type of backing-up step near the end of the song and use particular arm and hand movements. Then they proceed forward again, until the song ends.

LINDA J. GOODMAN first began her Ph.D. research in 1974 with a musical study of the Makah tribe. She met and became friends with Helma Swan (Ward at that time), and since 1979 the two have been working intermittently on Helma's life story with special emphasis on the place of music in her life. Formerly Dr. Goodman taught ethnomusicology at Colorado College (1975–86), was coordinator of education and public programs at the Museum of Indian Arts and Culture, Santa Fe (1987–89), and since 1989 has been employed as an ethnohistorian in the Office of Archaeological Studies at the Museum of New Mexico, in Santa Fe.

Since 1980 HELMA SWAN has been employed as a teacher and researcher at the Makah Cultural and Research Center, Neah Bay, Washington, where she consults for museum exhibits and cultural events. She continues to sing at a variety of Indian ceremonies and various non-Indian celebrations throughout the Northwest.

Native Music of the Pacific Northwest

A Washington State Perspective

LORAN OLSEN

AS WE EXPLORE THE MUSIC IN USE TODAY BY NATIVE AMERICANS in the state of Washington, it is necessary to be aware of the long history of exchange and interaction among the peoples of the Pacific Northwest. Not only were permanent villages located along the Strait of Juan de Fuca, the inland waterways of Puget Sound, the western Cascade rivers, the Olympic Peninsula streams, the mighty Columbia, and its many inland tributaries, but great trade routes followed these corridors as well. Such patterns of commerce fostered relationships among separate groups of indigenous people well before the time of the first European contact—relationships that continue to the present day.

Waterways provided the only easy access to Washington's coastal regions. The exploitation of water and forest resources made for a lifestyle of shared abundance among families, villages, and larger communities. In this region of plenty, the people developed complex ceremonial, religious, and social activities reflecting their proximity to the forces of nature and their human interdependence. Today's arbitrary boundaries do not reflect the interaction that water travel promoted in the past.

Music—song and dance—has been central to the lives of western Washington people and their neighbors since time immemorial. Music was employed in public displays for the upholding of chiefly power; in rites of passage; in secret societies; and during healing, travel, whaling, fishing, hunting, warfare, and recreation. Music also reflects the changes that came to these people after contact with Europeans, and today it reverberates with remnants from the past and elements of the present.

The Columbia River Plateau encompasses all of eastern Washington. It is an isolated area nestled among mountain ranges, with abundant water and food resources including salmon, game, roots, and berries. Interior Salish speakers have inhabited the northern two-thirds of the region for millennia; immediately to the south, Sahaptin speakers shared with the Salish the serenity of these river highlands in relative peace. At the time of contact, these groups reflected communal interaction and the sharing of resources through trade. A vibrant ceremonial life included recurrent first-fruits feasts, intertribal summer gatherings, winter spirit dances, weddings, and wakes.

At present there are twenty-six Indian reservations in Washington alone, and many more in the adjacent states and British Columbia. Many dimensions of the music employed by Native peoples of this region are no longer available to us; fortunately, this book and recording give us a small glimpse of the extent and variety of songs once sung here. From the perspective of the First People, music is more than the reiteration of instrumental or vocal repertoire for the purposes of perfection, entertainment, or self-expression. Song and dance have served as prayers, accessories to the forces of nature, resources for healing, vehicles of prophecy, nonverbal languages, improvisational lessons, historical records, honoring devices, communitywide recreations, intertribal bonding agents, proofs of lineage, and personal gifts of the highest value.

Music of the Northwest Coast

In the early 1800s, entrepreneurs near the mouth of the Columbia River spoke an accessible and functional trade language called Chinook Jargon, combining Chinookan and neighboring Indian tongues with English and French words. Reflecting such mixtures, sacred and secular Jargon songs sprang into use (Boas 1888), and some are still sung today.

Farther up the Olympic Peninsula coast, music was used as important property. The persistence with which the Quinault, Queets, Quileute, and Makah of the Olympic Peninsula and the Nootka of Vancouver Island's west coast would dance to their family songs at public occasions ensured them continued possession rights to these valued resources. Painted blankets, rattles, shredded cedar bark headdresses, wooden carved masks, and elaborate dance aprons—all part of the opulence—were requisite adjuncts to music and dance. Songs were used as significant gifts among

Kami San Tie Nok and wife Josephine, Wenatchi, ca. 1905.
Photograph courtesy of Robert Eddy

wealthy Makah and Nootkan chiefs, and served as memorable dowry items for noble marriages. To knowledgeable elders, they were legal and historical proof of a great person's lineage, material wealth, and chieftainship.

Long before European contact, the Straits Salish and Puget Sound Salish held spirit dances in large cedar smokehouses throughout the winter. Youthful initiates traveled all season to distant locations, reiterating new spiritual songs acquired in the practices of self-deprivation and separation from family, as they prepared for adult life. These spirit dances still occur every weekend in wintertime. New initiates appear with their supporters at sites extending north from Washington's Skokomish River to Vancouver Island and the mainland nearby (Amoss 1978a). Ceremonial items utilized with dance included mountain-goat wool clothing, scallop-shell rattles, deer-hoof rattles, long-haired headdresses that hang about the wearer's face, evergreen wands, decorated hand drums, and "pop-eyed" red and white masks.

Among cultures based on oral traditions, the preservation of group identity through song and story was imperative for survival. Songs and dances carried from previous generations by the elders were passed to certain youngsters who demonstrated responsibility and a bent for memorizing. The people interacted directly with nature on a daily basis. Accession to the mysterious powers available was fostered among the young through individual spirit quests, secret society initiations, and winter spirit dances.

The education system was based on alertness of the senses, concentration, and imitation. Children copied their elders, birds, animals, and the sounds of nature. They memorized and reiterated stories and songs in a holistic approach in which melody, rhythm, style, and text were all absorbed. Personal songs remembered from vision quests might be used for success in fishing, whaling, hunting, root digging, warring, gambling, love, or the ability to provide for a family. They might prove valuable for spiritual protection to an individual in danger. Songs were integral to curing rituals.

The music consisted mostly of one melodic line sung solo or by a group, often accompanied by rattles and drums. In some instances, melodies unfolded in parallel fourths or even thirds. Songs were built of short phrases in irregular groupings, repeated a few times with slight changes. Primarily pentatonic, or five-pitched, most melodies employed a central recitation tone and sustained other pitches at important moments. Depending on its purpose, a song might use brief cryptic words surrounded by syllables we now term "vocables" (such as *hu, hu, hu*) for sustaining longer lines.

Percussion instruments included rattles made of wood carved in bird shapes; of

Yakama Indians, ca. 1915. *Courtesy of Washington State University Libraries,*
Historical Photograph Collections, neg. 77-023

scallop shells and the horns of elk and mountain sheep; of deer hooves; and even, among the Makah, of whale baleen. Hollowed log drums, bentwood box drums, plank drums, and wooden frame drums covered with elk or deer hide were employed. Beat patterns reflective of the vocal line might be steady throughout or might be complex combinations of twos and threes, emphasizing certain words or dance steps.

Coastal groups manufactured whistles of two hollowed-out pieces of wood joined together. These were often family-owned possessions that imitated the sounds of certain birds or animals and were blown from hidden locations during secret ceremonies to announce the presence of supernatural beings.

Dance costumes varied considerably, depending on the tribal group and the purpose of the dance. The Lummi might wear black overshirts decorated with tiny wooden war clubs or paddles; the Makah and Clallam might wear black and red dance shirts or cloth dresses and shawls with animal crests. Dipping, turning, and spinning dance steps often imitated animals or birds. The moves ranged from simple rhythmic gestures and bounces, with open hands turned upward in thanks, to frenzied solo dances demonstrating spirit possession, with intense scowls, trembling hands, crouching, leaping, and shouting.

Plateau Music of Eastern Washington

On the Columbia Plateau, children ten to fifteen years of age embarked on personal guardian spirit quests in order to gain life-supporting powers for their adult years. Each quest, enhanced by fasting, resulted in a personal power song bestowed on the youngster by a benign animal spirit. Certain medicine men or women seeking to be healers gathered additional songs through cumulative quest experiences as they grew older. Some religious songs and dances were given by spirits to prophets who died and returned to life, with messages for the welfare of the people. Some recreational songs were improvised or composed.

Seasonal renewals began with winter spirit dances such as the Jumping Dance, still held annually among traditional interior Salish people to publicly share the past year's joys and sorrows and to enter into the new year communally strengthened. These were followed by dances celebrating the end of winter, by spring and summer root feasts, by ceremonial acknowledgment of protocols for successful hunting and fishing in summer and fall, and by family sweathouse rituals for personal cleansing throughout the year.

Palouse tribe, near Pasco, Washington, ca. 1900. *Courtesy of Washington State University Libraries, Historical Photograph Collections, neg. 97-082*

Song marked the relationship between mother and baby before birth, and among caregivers and instructors it remained integral for the nurturing of children from birth through childhood. Naming, puberty, courtship, and marriage activities required vocal music, as did the grandparents' story-songs in legends, designed to impart lessons to the young. Death and the passing of one's being to the spirit world were also accompanied by song.

In some instances, clashes with the Plains Blackfeet or with the Great Basin Shoshone required retaliation. Plateau people sang and danced while preparing to make a foray against the enemy—recruiting members for a war party and singing farewell songs at their departure. Personal songs might protect the warriors in battle. Victory songs and scalp dances (or songs of mourning) immediately followed the return of the war party; at later celebrations, war leaders were likely to be honored and veterans remembered in public dances.

Recreational music occurred during summer gatherings, feasts, and pageants. A popular gambling game, called the stick game on the Plateau or bone game on the coast, is still prevalent throughout the region; it is a guessing game in which fast tapping rhythms accompany energetic vocal melodies. In most Plateau cultures there were few children's game-songs; they were encouraged to play their own versions of adult games and dances.

In most Native languages there is no word for "music." "Song" and "singing" are the closest counterparts. Solo song and group singing of one melody with occasional doubling at the octave are common. Although certain sacred songs were meant to be sung without instrumental accompaniment, others required percussion to supply a "heartbeat" or a rhythmic counterpoint to the voice. Plateau percussion instruments included rattles of deer hooves or of rawhide-enclosed pebbles. As a rhythm instrument to support dancing, the rasp or notched stick preceded the hand drum among several Plateau groups. Since motion was a natural response to song and pulse, Native people conceived of dance as an integral part of musical expression.

Before the time of European contact, the standard melody instrument used on the Plateau was the end-blown flute with six finger holes. Flutes were most commonly made of elderberry wood or bird wingbone (later even of metal gun barrels), and smaller single-pitch whistles were fabricated of any convenient tubular material (Olsen 1979).

Most music from this region is pentatonic (five-toned), nontempered (not tuned in the conventional manner), monophonic (single melody) song. The vocal quality traditionally was varied, depending on the song's function. Mellow vocal styles were employed in love songs and in flute imitations of those love songs.

Wanapum Root Feast. *Courtesy of Washington State University Libraries, Historical Photograph Collections, neg. 97-021*

High-pitched, driving styles were used by drummer-singers to reach out over large groups of people or to lead dancers. Although some melodies carried texts, many employed vocables, such as *a, hey, ya, o, yo, ha*. As among the Plains Indians, Plateau singers added a pulsed drum accompaniment to a vocal line, often resulting in a composite polyrhythm, such as drumming in duples while singing in triples. Improvisational techniques included repeating, expanding, and reordering the notes of short motives and grouping some musical phrases in nonsymmetric patterns.

Today's Legacy

European and Euro-American explorers, traders, trappers, missionaries, settlers, and miners each brought novel types of music and musical instruments to the Native people of Washington. Although some combinations resulted, such as Christian hymns translated into Native languages, or English words sung to Native tunes, the two strains of musical expression—Native American and European—remained fundamentally separate.

Protestant missionaries arriving among the Nez Perce speakers in the late 1830s immediately set about developing a church-song literature in the native language. Among the first books ever printed in the Northwest is Henry Harmon Spalding's 1842 Nez Perce hymnal from the Mission Press of Lapwai, Idaho. Catholic Jesuit missionaries soon followed, translating into Salish additional songs and hymns, and introducing ritual and European musical instruments (Peterson 1993).

In 1882 and 1883 at the southern end of Puget Sound a new Nativistic-Christian religion was born among the Squaxin people, employing full-voiced hymn-like Salish song, stomping rhythms, handbells, altars, candles, healing, and shaking—a singular combination of the old and the new. Relying on revelation rather than the printed scripture, John and Mary Slocum's Indian Shaker Church spread swiftly over much of the Northwest and as far south as California (Gunther 1949). Many such congregations persist today throughout the Pacific Northwest, maintaining an intense and active song tradition.

Renewal ceremonies of thanksgiving have always marked the return of the salmon, celebrated the sharing of vegetal foods, placated the spirits of land and sea mammals who sustain human life, and reverenced the forces of creation for the gift of the cedar tree. Native Americans in the Pacific Northwest still hold festivals, naming ceremonies, worship services, wakes, feasts, dances, competitions, games, and annual celebrations of renewal—all central to their contemporary culture. Singing, drumming, and dancing have flourished, reflecting the vitality of oral traditions in song and story.

LORAN OLSEN is professor emeritus of music and Native American studies at Washington State University. With degrees from Grinnell, Drake, and the University of Iowa, Dr. Olsen has performed and lectured throughout the Midwest, Northwest, Alaska, and Canada. He has served as consultant and reviewer for several state and federal arts and humanities agencies. Among his publications, which include compositions, articles, movies, videotapes, slide shows, and monographs, is the eighteen-tape Nez Perce Music Archive and its accompanying guide, and the "Music and Dance" article for the Plateau volume of the Smithsonian Institution's *Handbook of North American Indians*.

Song Traditions of the Indian Shaker Church

JAMES EVERETT CUNNINGHAM

AND PAMELA AMOSS

THE INDIAN SHAKER CHURCH IS AN INDIGENOUS RELIGIOUS movement, centered around charismatic revelation and spiritual healing, that traces its origins to the southern Puget Sound region in the late nineteenth century. Despite its name and some superficial similarities, the Shaker Church that spread throughout the West Coast is not connected with the East Coast New England Shakers founded by Mother Ann Lee. Songs have been central to the beliefs and practices of the Indian Shaker Church, from its inception to the present, providing impetus for its continued influence throughout the region.

Early History

Most Shakers have avoided written histories, preferring to pass on church history by word of mouth. All accounts, both written and oral, are in agreement that the Indian Shaker Church was founded in 1881 or 1882 by John Slocum, a Squaxin Indian who lived at Skookum Chuck near Olympia, Washington (Eells 1892, 1985; Reagan 1908, 1910; Buchanan 1914; Waterman 1922; Mooney 1896; Gunther 1949; Barnett 1957; Harmon 1965; Gould and Furukawa 1964; Valory 1966; Fitzpatrick 1968; Richen 1974; Amoss 1978b, 1982, 1990; Castile 1982).

John Slocum, ca. 1890, possibly at the first Shaker church at Mud Bay near Olympia.
Photographer unknown; courtesy of University of Washington Libraries,
Erna Gunther Papers, Manuscripts and Archives Division, neg. 543-9912

Rare early photograph of Mary Slocum, wife of John Slocum and first to receive the
gift of the "shake." *Photographer unknown; courtesy of University of Washington Libraries,
Erna Gunther Papers, Manuscripts and Archives Division, neg. 543-1929*

The propensity for oral tradition, however, has yielded many variations of the actual circumstances surrounding the beginnings of the Indian Shaker Church. All accounts are in general agreement that John Slocum returned from the dead with a prophetic message from God, instructing him to build a church and preach, urging the Indian people to give up the vices they had learned from non-Indians, namely drinking and smoking. They were also to abstain from traditional practices of spirit dancing, Indian doctoring, and gambling. In return, he said, God promised to send a "medicine" to heal the Indians.

As the word of his miraculous return from the dead and his message of hope and salvation spread, John Slocum developed an early following among local Indians who gathered at his church on Mud Bay, near Olympia, to worship with him. Little is known about these early services, except that they combined ritual elements borrowed from Catholic, Protestant, and indigenous religious practices (Barnett 1957: 285–307; Castile 1982). About a year after his first revelation, John Slocum succumbed to a second illness, which by some accounts he had brought upon himself by gambling. When his father insisted on sending for an Indian doctor, John's wife Mary ran from the house overcome by grief and anxiety. As she cried alone at a nearby creek, a song came to her, the singing of which caused her hands to tremble violently (Barnett 1957:25, 33). Spiritually empowered, she returned to the house and miraculously cured her husband.

Mary Slocum's healing gift was interpreted as the "medicine" promised by God to John in his original prophesy. Her ecstatic trembling became known as the "shake," from which the religion gets its name. Other believers followed Mary as recipients of the gift of the shake, and the fledgling Shaker Church spread rapidly to other Indian communities—north into British Columbia, east to Idaho, and south through Oregon and into northern California—alarming some local officials.

Because of the political and religious pressure by governmental agents and Christian missionaries, the early Shakers were compelled to seek legal counsel. A sympathetic non-Indian attorney, James Wickersham, advised them of their legal right "to worship in any peaceful manner they chose" (Barnett 1957:59). In 1910 the Indian Shaker Church became a legally incorporated religion under the laws of Washington State, with the assistance of Milton Giles, a justice of the peace at Olympia. The original charter of the Indian Shaker Church established a political structure similar to Protestant churches of the period, with a bishop, a board of elders, ministers, and missionaries (Barnett 1957:110–13).

Purpose, Membership, and Setting

Since its earliest days, the healing of mind, body, and soul has been the main mission of the Shaker religion. To this day, Shakers take their responsibility to heal suffering very seriously and will minister to anyone who asks them. So strong is this obligation that active Shakers may be on the road every weekend to bring their healing work to Shakers and non-Shakers, both Indian and non-Indian alike. Shakers never ask for payment for their services. All they expect and will accept are meals, and perhaps a little money to pay for gas. Because of their generosity and commitment, Shakers are highly respected in local Indian communities, where they carry far greater influence than their small numbers would suggest. A 1974 study of the Shaker population showed less than a thousand individuals (Richen 1974:13). A similar study today would probably indicate fewer.

Membership in a particular Shaker congregation is filled by Indians from the immediate area, with the occasional non-Indian member. A hierarchy exists in each community in the form of appointed offices, such as minister or elder. However, the work of church members is not guided by official rank, but focuses on the strength and purpose of individual gifts received from God and shared with others. The power to shake, and thereby to heal, is given to each Shaker according to his or her disposition to receive it, but congregational unanimity is essential to successful work—whether curing, inspiring a convert, or cleansing a "sinner" of an addiction.

Harmony within the congregation must be mirrored by harmony within the homes of the members. Just as the revelations given to John Slocum and the gift of the shake given to Mary Slocum contributed equally to the conception of the Shaker church, contemporary Shakers assign equal and complementary roles to women and men. The participation of each spouse is vital because men and women, working together, complement each other, creating a harmonious team. Shakers who are at odds with family members, especially those at cross-purposes with their spouses, may not receive the power of the Spirit or utilize its full potential.

The Articles of Incorporation of the Shaker Church of Washington, drafted in 1910 by Milton Giles, state that one of the objectives of the church is "the elevation of the female Indian, they to be equal in the government of the church" (Barnett 1957: 111). Although more men than women have been elected or appointed to formal leadership positions, both sexes are equally active as preachers, healers, and missionaries. Equal roles for men and women are mirrored by equal musical participation.

Indian Shaker church built by the Clallam Indians at Jamestown, 1905. *Courtesy of University of Washington Libraries, Edmond S. Meany Albums, vol. 3, leaf 28, neg.* NA-1173a

Preaching and healing are done in the church buildings that can be seen on or near Indian reservations throughout the Pacific Northwest, and are the most visible signs of the continued existence of the Shaker faith. The first churches that were built just before the turn of the century have undergone little change. On the outside many are indistinguishable from old rural Christian churches; plain rectangular buildings, with modest belfries. One local Indian Shaker Church, on the Tulalip Indian Reservation near Marysville, Washington, received international attention in the early 1990s when it was used as a set for the "Northern Exposure" television series in exchange for badly needed repairs.

Inside Shaker churches a simple altar or "prayer table" is placed near the end of the room opposite the door, with a large wooden cross hung on the wall above. In a few churches, the prayer table is set in a small niche directly under the belfry. The prayer table is covered with a white cloth on which are placed candles used during the services and handbells to accompany songs. Although many churches now have electricity, lighting for services is provided exclusively by the candles on the prayer table, in candelabras hanging from the ceiling, and in wall sconces. Unlike Christian churches, with rows of pews, the floor area of a Shaker church is normally open, with benches along the walls. During the service a few chairs may be placed in the middle of the room, facing the prayer table, to accommodate sick people there to seek help. Every devout Shaker also has a small prayer table with a cross, candles, and handbells in his or her house. There, individual Shakers pray in the morning and the evening, and the family, with perhaps a few friends, can gather for private services.

The Concept of Song

Song has been an integral part of the Indian Shaker Church since the earliest services conducted by John Slocum, and song has remained central to the Shaker faith and to the everyday life of individual Shakers. Songs are sung during Sunday church services, in smaller services held in the homes of Shakers, and at nighttime curing rituals called "shakes"—held either in churches or in private homes if the infirm are too ill to travel. Shakers also sing for blessings before and after meals and during special occasions such as funerals and birthday celebrations. They also sing informally at home or while traveling, to gain strength and satisfaction.

Shaker songs are considered sacred because they are seen as originating directly from the Spirit of God. Their sanctity is further enhanced because Shakers also view songs as prayers or a means of communicating directly with God (Olsen 1979; Vi Hilbert, personal communication). In keeping with their practices of avoiding written history and the use of written scripture, Shakers have also avoided formal musical composition, notation, and analysis. Their songs have been received, sung, remembered, and passed on from the beginnings of the Indian Shaker Church to the present solely through oral tradition. A current member of the Indian Shaker Church said that it was incorrect to consider Shaker songs as music, because the term "music" has a secular connotation that is out of place in the sacred context of all Shaker songs. Although Shakers resist categorization of their songs, they appear to conceptualize them in three ways: first, in terms of *efficacy*; second, in terms of *ownership* and *origin*; and lastly, in terms of *purpose*.

Efficacy Of Songs

One of the most important determiners of a Shaker song is its efficacy, or its "power to produce an effect." For a Shaker, God's presence in a song is something tangible that can be both felt and witnessed. A local Shaker said he could distinguish between Shaker songs and other types of Indian songs, not acoustically, but because he could "feel the power [of God's Holy Spirit] in it." The efficacy of Shaker songs is also evident in the physical effects they produce. To a Shaker, the trembling of an individual's hands, which is activated through song, is proof of its divine source. To those undergoing the ministrations of the Shakers, the mental, physical, or spiritual healing that results from the shake is further evidence of its power. Many Indians have reported that the Shakers were able to help them with problems that resisted other forms of treatment. Shaker songs, then, are recognized by the feelings and reactions they evoke in the singers and hearers, as well as their direct and therapeutic effects.

Song Origin and Ownership

Song ownership is a characteristic of all Indian music in the Pacific Northwest (Herzog 1949). "Ownership" is defined as the recognized right to sing a particular song, that right belonging to the person who first received or composed it. An owned song can be given away, sold, or passed on through inheritance, often becoming the property of an entire family.

Despite slight regional and individual variations in the way that Shaker traditions are understood, there is general agreement that a Shaker song is not composed or made up, but is received as divine inspiration directly from the Holy Spirit of God. Some Shakers are known to have a "gift," a heaven-sent facility for receiving new songs, whereas others may participate faithfully for years before they receive a single song. In the Shaker tradition, the owner of a particular song is the one who first brings it out in public and teaches it to others. When a person sings a song for the first time at a Shaker service, the rest of the congregation soon learns it and joins in whenever the originator sings it. From that time on, it becomes the recognized property of that individual and is not usually sung unless its "owner" is present (Rhodes 1974:181). However, there is an important distinction between the ownership of Shaker and other indigenous songs in the Pacific Northwest; since Shaker songs ultimately come from God, they belong to their "owner" in name only and cannot be sold.

After a while, a particular song might be sung by others out of the presence of its "owner," although it remains known as that individual's song. Over time, people may forget who first received the song and it moves into the public domain, becoming part of the general treasury of the Shaker song tradition. Visitors from other Shaker congregations throughout the West Coast can also learn the songs, and take them home with them. In this manner individual Shaker songs travel great distances. This pattern of song ownership is consistent with many traditional song types in the Pacific Northwest, including gambling and family songs.

Native people from western Washington and southeastern British Columbia, where the Spirit Dancing religion is still active, recognize the clear parallels between the pattern of Shakers receiving songs from the Holy Spirit and Spirit Dancers receiving songs from their guardian spirits. Although both are considered proof of contact with the supernatural, there are two important differences between the origin and ownership of Shaker and guardian spirit songs. First, Shaker songs are gifts from God, not a guardian spirit; second, whereas Spirit Dancers' songs are individually received and exclusively owned, Shaker songs are individually received but may eventually become communally owned.

Purposes of Songs

Most often, Shakers view songs according to their purpose, or how they are used. Although the same song may be sung in a variety of circumstances, many Shaker songs have a specific power that enables the recipient to perform a particular job. Thus, specific songs are sung for bringing the gift of the shake to new devotees, while others are for healing, worship, or to console people in mourning. Many songs are sung to lift or "lighten" the spirits, and may be sung at any time, while doing physical labor, at home, or when traveling.

Song is the conduit that connects each Shaker with the power of the Holy Spirit of God. When a would-be Shaker comes to the church, he or she is expected to stand up before the prayer table during an evening shake and wait to receive the power that manifests itself through involuntary shaking. How long it takes for the power to move the new joiner varies with each individual. Some new joiners must stand up for as long as four nights before they receive the power. Certain Shakers have special songs to invite the power to help a new joiner "get the shake" (receive the gift of the shake). Singing these songs not only helps the new joiners begin to shake, but also intensifies the vigor with which experienced Shakers receive their shaking power.

As previously noted, it was a specific song that preceded Mary Slocum's first receipt of the shake. When others joined the early church, they too received songs as well as the healing gift of the shake. The charisma of the shake was a primary reason that the Indian Shaker Church had such initial appeal, and has contributed to its longevity.

Shakers refer to spiritual healing as "work." Because of the emphasis on healing as a primary mission of the church, "work songs" comprise a major part of the Shaker song repertoire. During a shake, the infirm come forward and sit in the chairs that have been placed for them in front of the prayer table. Shakers in attendance surround the sick and brush or rub the ill person's body with their shaking hands, meanwhile passing the flame of the candles near the supplicant, as they sing and move rhythmically to the beat of the handbells. In this manner the illness, sin, or sorrow is removed from the patient and held in the cupped hands of the attending Shakers, who dispel it by throwing it at the cross, releasing it into the flame of a candle, or tossing it out the church door (Gunther 1949:59). The atmosphere created by these songs, in combination with the ritual setting, focuses both the healers' and the sufferer's attention on the healing process. In such a setting, the songs, like the bells, the light from the candles, and the ministrations of the helpers, symbolize the power of God mobilized to heal and inspire.

Singing, as an act of devotion, has been intimately connected with the Indian Shaker Church since its beginning. The relationship between song and prayer is so close "that one is obliged to regard them as complementary elements of a larger complex" (Rhodes 1974:181). During John Slocum's first services, anyone could stand and either pray or sing aloud as an act of faith (Barnett 1957:238). In modern times, weekly Shaker worship services, held on Sunday mornings, are formal occasions on which many of the congregation wear their distinctive white robes with appliquéd blue crosses. Sunday services include an inspirational sermon, personal testimonials, prayers, and hymn singing. They conclude with the simultaneous recitation by the entire congregation of individual prayers and songs, in both Indian dialects and English. Although not considered song per se, the polyphonic and charismatic blend of diverse melodies and spoken language by many individual Shakers creates a "strikingly beautiful choral effect" (Rhodes 1974:181). Services in Shaker homes have the same format as Sunday services with devotional hymn singing and prayer, but omit the sermon.

Musical Analysis

Even though song is integral to the practice of the Shaker faith, ethnographies of the Indian Shaker Church make only sporadic reference to music and no analysis of musical style. Nor does Shaker music receive any mention in regional and areal studies of Northwest Coast Indian music, possibly because it has not been seen as a "pure" form of indigenous expression (Eells 1879; Roberts and Haeberlin 1918; Roberts 1936; Herzog 1949; Nettl 1954). Up to the present, the only published study of Shaker music is a short article written by ethnomusicologist Willard Rhodes as a part of a larger study of North American Indian music for the Bureau of Indian Affairs (1974:180–84).

As a basis for his analysis of Shaker music, Rhodes recorded twenty-nine Shaker songs in various locations throughout western Washington in the summer of 1950. Four of those songs, sung by Tommy Bob on the Swinomish Reservation near La Conner, were included on the commercially available record album, *Music of the American Indian: Northwest (Puget Sound)* (Rhodes 1954). Rhodes included only a brief mention of Shaker music in the accompanying liner notes. It was not until 1974 that he published the findings of his earlier study, in which he identified "Shaker songs as a distinct song type . . . [with] a homogeneity of style" (Rhodes 1974:182).

The following analysis of the Shaker musical style is based on the Rhodes study and on recordings of Shaker songs collected by Rhodes in 1950, Leon Metcalf in 1952 and 1961, and Vivian Williams in 1962; on contemporary recordings of Shaker services in northern California and Puget Sound; and on personal experience. Songs, collected over more than four decades, show a surprising continuity, illustrating the consistency of the Shaker song tradition. Due to the personal nature of song acquisition, any analysis, even that based on a large body of material, is a generalization and therefore not necessarily applicable to all Shaker songs.

Vocal Style

Consistent with most Indian music throughout North America, the Shaker song tradition is purely vocal. No melodic instruments are used; the few instruments that are used function exclusively as rhythmic accompaniment to song. Therefore, vocal style "serves as an [important] identifying feature" of Shaker songs (Rhodes 1974:182). The Shaker vocal style has many similarities to the Salish musical tradition of the Pacific Northwest, which is distinct when compared with the vocal style found in much of Native North America.

The Shaker vocal style can be best described as open and relaxed, with the frequent use of a pronounced vibrato or "shaking" quality of the voice. The vocal range, or tessitura, of Shaker songs is typically in the middle register for both men and women. These features contrast directly with the vocal tension created by a restriction of the vocal chords and high tessitura employed in the Plains vocal style, typical of the modern powwow tradition.

Shaker songs are often punctuated with prominent gasps, which were described by Rhodes as "deep, heavy, audible inhalations" (1974:181). These gasps occur between the short sung phrases, when the singers allow their vocal chords to vibrate when they take in air. Since breath intake is usually unvocalized, the fact that such audible breathing can be heard in Shaker songs is significant and should be viewed as an integral part of the sonic complex.

Although some Shaker songs sound like Christian hymns, the similarities can be misleading, because the Shaker songs are also similar to other types of indigenous musical expression that predate Christian influence. Much in the same way that the Shaker religion combines ritual elements from both Christian and indigenous traditions, the Shaker vocal style syncretizes musical elements from these disparate sources.

Melody, Dynamics, and Harmony

Aside from analysis of vocal style, Shaker songs can be divided into two categories based on types of melody. Some closely resemble Christian hymns, and others have melodies similar to traditional Indian songs. Rhodes wrote that "the influence of Christian gospel hymns on the Shakers songs is obvious," and theorized that fragments of Christian hymns were borrowed and combined with other melodic elements to form new songs. This is consistent with the way that new songs are developed throughout the Northwest. He also noted that "the pendulum movement and the use of wide jumps, noted in most of the Shaker material, as well as the less frequent 'broken-chord' pattern, are traits of Salish music" (1974:183).

The expressive quality of Shaker songs is most evident in terms of dynamics. Songs are typically loudest at the beginning of a verse. From that point on, the volume gradually decreases throughout until reaching the lowest dynamic level at verse's end. When the verse is repeated or a new one is begun, the volume soars, and along with it the enthusiasm of the singer(s), giving each verse in succession a wave-like ebb and flow quality as it shifts from loud to soft.

As is true of most vocal traditions throughout Native North America, Shaker songs are monophonic, with men and women singing in unison on the same pitch or at the octave. Their combined voices blend together, creating an almost seamless melody. One can infer that unity in the singing of Shaker songs mirrors the interaction and cooperation between men and women in the Shaker faith.

Rhodes reports "occasional examples of heterophony [in Shaker songs], so rare in North American Indian music"; however, slight variances between several singers of the same song can be as easily attributed to individual variation as to a feature of musical style (1974:182). Because of the strict unison singing in the Shaker tradition, there is an absence of Western harmony as found in Christian hymns, and there is no evidence of the unique parallel harmony or call-and-response that can be heard in the traditional guardian spirit and *slahal* gambling songs of the Pacific Northwest Indians.

Form

Shaker songs vary greatly from one to another and are not tied to any strict form or internal structure, but do have some similarities. Songs normally consist of one verse of two, three, or four short phrases (with a preference for the three-phrase pattern) that are repeated indefinitely (Rhodes 1974:181–82). Typically, a song is begun spontaneously by one individual, who sings the first verse alone in a slow and deliberate manner. Others then join in on the second repetition, as soon as they recognize the song, or "catch the melody" if it is unfamiliar. The song is repeated indefinitely until the person who started it is moved to end it or to begin another. It is very common for three or more songs to be strung together in this manner, with each one blending into the next, creating a set or suite of songs without a distinguishable break (Rhodes 1974). So smooth is the transition from one song to the next, that it may be difficult or impossible to tell when one song ends and another begins.

Since Shakers believe that all songs come directly from God, he is the ultimate source of their form, length, and the order in which they are sung. When Rhodes asked Mrs. Jessie Moses of Marblemount, Washington, to sing one song at a time during a recording session, "she replied that she could not do that because she had to sing the songs as they were given to her [by God]" (1974:181).

Accompaniment

The most obvious and distinctive identifier of Shaker songs is the rhythmic accompaniment provided by brass handbells, played in pairs, and which vary "in size, the average being that of the old country school bell with which the teacher signaled the class" (Rhodes 1974:180). Handbells have been an integral part of the Shaker faith since its inception. John Slocum first used a handbell to call his followers to worship and to signal the different sections during his early services. Mary Slocum first introduced handbells as accompanying instruments when she sang and shook over John to cure him of his second, fatal illness (Barnett 1957:210). Both functions of the bells are alive today in the practices of the Indian Shaker Church.

In the past, bells were played only by men, but at present many women possess bells and participate as bell ringers during services and shakes (Barnett 1957:209; Rhodes 1974:180). Shakers who are without bells may also provide rhythmic accompaniment by clapping their hands. The drums, rattles, and other percussion instruments which accompany traditional Indian music throughout the Northwest have not been adopted by the Shakers, because they avoid all accouterments connected with other Native belief systems.

The handbells provide a steady rhythm, which matches the melody and highlights the minimal use of syncopation in Shaker songs (Rhodes 1974:182). The main pulse of the bells, produced by the motion of the players' wrists as they swing the bells up and down, can be subdivided into two beats—alternating short and long, and loud and soft. During a song, the tempo typically begins slow (60 to 70 beats per minute) and gradually increases until it reaches about 120 beats per minute by the end of the song (Rhodes 1974:181–82).

The bell ringing often continues between songs, further obscuring the transition from one song to the next. The leader may slow the tempo when beginning a new song, which will again build toward a climax. In this manner there is a constant tension and release from one song to the next throughout the evening. The ringing tones of the bells also produce a clear, strong, continuous overtone that can be heard over the voices of the singers.

Shakers all move in time to the bells, with a stylized stomping of their feet on the hard wooden floor of the church. Although referred to as "dance" in some sources, the stomping is not considered dance by the Shakers (Gunther 1949:52; Reagan 1908). Termed "following the bells" and performed en masse either in place or around the interior of the church in a counterclockwise direction, this deliberate stomping movement blends with the bell ringing as a rhythmic accompaniment to song. Barnett writes, "Keeping their elbows bent, they proceed to bring the bells up and down in front of them and at the same time stamp the rhythm with their heels as heavily as their enthusiasm dictates. As the fervor spreads, the noise rises in a deafening crescendo. The floor resounds and vibrates with the added tread of the Shakers, and after an hour or more of this mass movement the walls themselves seem to pulsate to the rhythm" (1957:209).

With rhythmic stomping as an accompaniment for Shaker songs, the church building itself becomes a musical instrument. Although Shakers deny any relation between their songs and other indigenous music traditions, they do preserve the ancient practice of using structures as percussion instruments. During potlatches and winter ceremonials throughout the Northwest coast, it was common for ceiling beams and roof planks of communal houses to be pounded by long poles or "drumming sticks" to accompany song (Smith 1940:117–18). Also, from a purely sonic perspective, the sound of the rhythmic stomping by Shakers is very reminiscent of the booming resonance of the hand drums used to accompany guardian spirit or *slahal* songs.

Text

The Shaker songs whose melodies resemble old Protestant or Catholic hymns often have English text or contain words borrowed from Chinook Jargon or local Indian languages. Most commonly sung as praise or prayer songs during Sunday morning services, they do not have the verse-refrain form used in most Christian hymns. As previously mentioned, they usually consist of one or more short verses that are repeated over and over again as exemplified in the following text:

> How can you meet Jesus,
> If you are not true?
> How can you meet Jesus?
> (Gunther 1949:55)

The text of this song, and many others with English words, shows borrowing from the Protestant hymn tradition in its reference to meeting Jesus. The translation of John Slocum's prayer song, although sung in his native language, shows a similar structure and thematic borrowing:

> *O Sha-ak tca-tl*
> *Aas kwa a-hwa-to-mo-tle*

> *Tu-hwal ti Sli-tca tli*, etc.
> *Tu-hwal sa-u-ha-li-tca tle*, etc.
> *Klo-hoi tca-tl ha li*, etc.
>
> Oh God, our Father above
> Help us always
> As long as life lasts
> Until we have life hereafter
> Through God our Father.
> (Eells 1985:440)

Spontaneous exclamations, such as "Praise the Lord," "Massee," and "Amen," also occur frequently during the singing of Shaker songs (Rhodes 1974:181). Although they are seen as extraneous to the original text and are randomly voiced by anyone present when moved through exuberance (usually at the end of phrases), these exhortations should be viewed as an integral part of each song.

Shaker songs with vocable texts are most often sung as work or healing songs at shakes. It is these songs that most closely resemble the older Indian traditional musical style (Barnett 1957; Gunther 1949). Vocables such as *ha, na, he, yo,* and *ho* are very common in North American indigenous music, but have often been called "nonsense syllables," thus demeaning their significance. A more proper definition for vocables is syllables without known lexical meaning. In reality, vocables *are* the words of a song, with the same vocables being used in the same place each time a song is sung.

Although a variety of vocables are used in Shaker songs, both Gunther and Rhodes report that the vocable *hai* (pronounced "high") is a marker of Shaker songs, because of its frequent and exclusive use (Gunther 1949:52; Rhodes 1974:182). *Hai* also appears as a refrain at the end of phrases in Shaker songs that contain words, such as in this Shaker song, recorded by Rhodes in 1950:

> God be with you
> Wherever you go,
> If you follow His ways in truth, *hai,*
> And God be with you,
> God be with you, *hai-i-hai.*
>
> —*Shaker Prayer Song, sung by Hannah Bowechop,*
> *recorded in Neah Bay, Washington, August 29, 1950*

Conclusion

Because the Indian Shaker Church successfully incorporated the Christian doctrine of a benevolent deity with traditional practices and beliefs, it has been a continuing force for both change and conservation of indigenous religious ideals in the Northwest. During its early history, the Shaker Church motivated local Indians to adapt to the demands of an ever-encroaching Western society, while allowing them an outlet for the preservation of their Indian identity. In the 115 years since its inception, and because of the spiritual devotion and giving nature of the Shakers themselves, the church has become integral to the indigenous culture of the Pacific Northwest. To-day, the Indian Shaker Church remains influential throughout the region by continuing to provide spiritual energy for the healing of both social and personal ills.

The song traditions of the Indian Shaker Church, so central to its beliefs and practices, have paralleled the continuing influence of the church in the Pacific Northwest. Taken as a whole, Shaker songs represent a specific genre of contemporary Native music, created by combining musical elements borrowed and adapted from Christian hymn singing, indigenous Indian song traditions, and other sources. The Shaker song tradition directly reflects the syncretic composition of the Indian Shaker Church, which combines disparate ideological and symbolic elements into new forms. The songs themselves, individually received but communally sung, exist as models of the individuality, high personal standards, and devotion to community that make the Indian Shaker Church a vital part of the heritage of the Pacific Northwest.

JAMES EVERETT CUNNINGHAM received his Ph.D. in ethnomusicology from the University of Washington, and he has instructed in the American Indian Studies Department there since 1992. He wrote his dissertation on *slahal*, a traditional Indian gambling game still played in western Washington, Vancouver Island, and mainland British Columbia.

PAMELA AMOSS received her Ph.D. from the Department of Anthropology at the University of Washington, where she also served on the faculty. She is the author of *Coast Salish Spirit Dancing* and the article on the Indian Shaker Church in volume 7 of the Smithsonian series *Handbook of North American Indians*. She continues to do research and writing on Northwest Natives, and does contract work as an applied anthropologist.

Songs from the Coast, Sound, and Plateau

Native American Music Traditions in Washington Today

WILLIE SMYTH

DESPITE SOCIAL AND CULTURAL UPHEAVAL AND PRESSURE TO abandon their traditions, members of Washington tribes have retained much music, mostly in its original form, and it remains an essential part of Indian life. Religious and social songs make up the principal singing traditions. Many of the religious songs are owned by individuals, families, or groups, and are thus protected somewhat from public presentation. The social songs are, however, available to a wider audience. The accompanying recording contains a sampling of the diverse song traditions which can be found throughout the state—from welcoming songs (Paddle Song, track 8), social dance songs (Owl and Willow Songs, tracks 11 and 12), and lullabies; to game songs (tracks 6 and 17), honor songs (track 15), love songs (T'abaa Song, track 5), and religious songs (tracks 3 and 9).

Note: This chapter was compiled by Willie Smyth with assistance from Loran Olsen, Joan Rabinowitz, Rebecca Chamberlain, and Jens Lund. Rebecca Chamberlain collected the fieldnotes and translated and transliterated all music selections except track 1 (by Bruce-*subiyay* Miller), track 5 (by Linda J. Goodman), track 18 (by Thomas E. Connolly), and tracks 19, 20, 21 (by Fred Hill, Sr.). Further assistance was given to Rebecca by Vi [taqʷšəblu] Hilbert, Bruce-*subiyay* Miller, Johnny Moses, Virginia Beavert, Pauline Hillaire, Elaine Emerson, and Lillian Pullen.

The singers on this recording (see Plates 14-23) were all recognized by tribal members as exemplary representatives who are keeping song traditions alive in their communities.

Western Washington

1. Chinook Changer Song. Bruce-*subiyay* Miller, Skokomish

Bruce-*subiyay* Miller is a noted artist, ceremonial leader, and teacher from the Skokomish Nation near Shelton. Originally, the name "Skokomish" referred to a community of Twana-speaking people who lived along the Skokomish River and its north fork. In translation, Skokomish means "people of the big river." The Skokomish were one of at least nine separate *tuwaduq*-speaking villages who collectively called themselves *tuwaduq*, anglicized as Twana.

This song, which came to *subiyay* spiritually, is about the cultural hero named *dukʷibəł* (Transformer) who changed the world into its present form. It is sung, as many old songs were, in Chinook Jargon. Chinook Jargon is a limited trade language comprised of words contributed from Chinook, various Native dialects of the Pacific Northwest, French, and English.

As in all American Indian languages, Chinook must be used in a metaphorical context. To try to use it in a literal sense, as English is used, is impossible. The Changer Song is an example of this metaphorical interpretive logic. The words are as follows:

Chako neewah dukʷibəł (pause) *massi* (two times)
konaway tum tum huy huy alta

METAPHORICAL TRANSLATION

chako	come, arrive, approach, become fulfilled destiny
neewah	here, this place, hither
dukʷibəł	(pronounced 'du kwee bahl') the Transformer
massi	thanks, rejoicing
konaway	everything in creation, the entirety
tum tum	heart, soul, true belief, feeling, conviction
huy huy	exchanged, fixed, agreed, traded
alta	now, right here and now, this moment

In the Changer Song, the translation thus approximates the following:

chako "the prophesied (second) arrival of the Transformer who will restructure the
world again"—a similar concept to the second coming of Christ, and all the
terminologies that apply to that event
neewah "the prophesied time"—the present time and space, the here and now
massi "thankfulness and rejoicing"—everything that is related to these concepts
konaway "every possible thing that exists"—everything in creation; the universe
tum tum "there will be total accord or harmony (in the universe)"
huy huy "(total harmony will be) by mutual consent"
alta "here we are now in the midst of that (long ago prophesied) time"

> *chako neewah dukʷibəɬ . . . massi*
> *konoway tum tum huy huy alta*
> *ho wee oh ho* (two times)
> *ho yu wee ah ho ho*
> *ho . . . wee lo*

2. The Thunderbird Song. Bruce-*subiyay* Miller, Skokomish

This song, as well as the preceding one, is a story-song, sung when people gather to
tell stories and to sing songs. They often feature legends; *subiyay* explains that this
one refers to:

a time among our people when there was great strife and famine in the land. They asked
the Great Spirit to send his son to help the people. When his son came, he was in the form
of the Thunderbird. He spread his teachings of *sqʷəlalitut* (spirit power) among our
people.

The rapid drumming is symbolic of the transformation of the Thunderbird from a
supernatural state into a human. After he came down, he traveled the earth sharing
sqʷəlalitut and *stu-kwy-yəth*—the prophesies and laws of harmony.

This song is made up of vocables, which *subiyay* says "carry the power of the song."
Vocables are very common in indigenous music throughout North America, but
have often been misidentified as "nonsense syllables." They are, in fact, the "words"
of the song, with the same vocables being used in the same place each time the song
is sung.

3. Indian Shaker Song. Johnny Moses, Tulalip

Johnny Moses, from the Tulalip Indian Reservation on the upper Puget Sound, is known across the state for his role in teaching and preserving Native cultural traditions. He has spent many years with relatives from the Clallam, Nootkas, Straits Salish, Puget Sound Salish, Yakama, and Spokane nations, reflecting his diverse cultural immersion and training. He learned this song among the Coast Salish Shakers, whom he joined after he was healed of cancer. The Native Shaker religion of the Pacific Northwest is explained in Chapter 9.

This is a healing song. Listen to the sound of the handbell played in rhythmic repetition for the Shaker service, which is accompanied by stomping in a counter-clockwise circle.

TRANSLATION

Giving thanks, let it be. / Toward the name of the Father / And of the Son / And of the Holy Spirit / That which is good—let it be.

> oh massi ʔistəʔ (*massi* here can also mean 'spirit')
>
> dxʷʔal kwi snaʔs mans
>
> ti te menaʔs
>
> ti te santus pli
>
> ƛ'um ʔəsʔistəʔ

4. Baby Teasing Song. Johnny Moses, Tulalip

This song, a *p'ip'ic'ikʷ* (diaper-changing) song, was learned from Johnny's grandmother, Jane Moses from the Tulalip Reservation, who learned it from *her* grandmother. It is a *sduhubš* (Snohomish) humorous teasing song sung by mothers when changing a baby's diaper. The song serves to soothe and distract the baby while it is being changed.

The song may be sung with three variations, the first to symbolize the mother carrying the child, the second to represent the mother and the unborn child singing to each other, and the third to signify the time after the baby is born. Most of the text consists of numerous vocables interspersed with occasional Lushootseed words, such as *dbədaʔ* (child), and *taɬ šədəb* (spread your feet). No exact translation is available, but the general gist of the song is: "No matter how messy you are, you are still beautiful."

ʔu yəƛəbili əʔ

hə da huy yə bə bə

bi yə buʔbi yə ha ha

(She would be rocking the baby on her knee)

ʔu hə bi yə

bə bi yə bə

he da da bə

hə da x̌ətx̌əɬ aʔdi

təɬ dbədaʔ yə

ɬu čuɬil dəʔbil

ʔu ʔu ɬuʔ swʔi təɬ sʔp'i p'i

dbədaʔ

hʔe ʔay ʔə ho

(Then she laid the baby down and said)

taɬ šədəb, taɬ šədəb.

5. T'abaa Song. Helma Swan, Makah

Helma Swan is an elder in the Makah Nation, where she has been very active in the protection and passing on of their language and culture. Helma, whose story is in Chapter 7, is the leader of her family dance group. Some of her family's dances have been handed down from generation to generation for more than 150 years. A few of their songs came from spiritual experiences, and others came to Helma's family through marriage and gifts or were learned at potlatches. The Makah are maritime people from the Pacific coast of the Olympic Peninsula.

In Helma's words: "The Makahs were very much a trading people. . . . They would trade up and down from California to Haida territory way up North. During this time, they would go into some of the potlatches. Maybe they would see one going on as they were traveling. When they came home, they mimicked the songs they heard there."

Helma learned this song from her father, who used to sing it often. It is a Makah love song in the category of social song called *T'abaa*. She says: "I heard that it was a song that one of the men started when he was missing his girlfriend or his wife. When you hear 'aiku-aiku,' that means 'I hurt, I hurt.'" The rest of the text is made up of vocables.

6. Bone Game Song. Helma Swan, Makah

Bone game songs are popular among American Indians across the country. Also known as stick games, hand games, or *slǝhal* (pronounced slah-hal; listen for it in the song), bone games are entertaining and informative expressions of traditional Native culture (see "The Origin of the Bone or Stick Game" in Chapter 2). Songs are integral to the game and some of the most lively American Indian songs have been, and still are, composed for this tradition. Thousands of bone game teams across the nation meet annually to play this gambling game and to sing and socialize.

Helma says of this song: "This is one of the bone game songs that they sometimes sing down by the beach at Neah Bay during celebrations. . . . I used to watch my dad. He'd throw the bones straight up, up and down. He used to roll his bones when he was singing. That's what the song says, 'My bones are flying. My bones are flying.' That's all it says. This is a real old one. Other tribes use the song, too, now. They're starting to, which they never did before. Even this is changed now. It's mixed up with different tongues—I sang it the old Makah way."

7. Lummi Chief's Song. Pauline Hillaire, Lummi

Pauline Hillaire has been teaching traditional Lummi songs and dances to family members and at the Northwest Indian College in Bellingham for several years. The Lummi, a people from an island in Bellingham Bay, are believed to have lived formerly on part of a group of islands east of Vancouver Island. Pauline learned most of her songs from her father, the late Joseph Hillaire, and has named her dance group the Setting Sun Dancers, after a group started earlier than the 1920s by her grandfather, Frank Hillaire. She recalls that he used to bring his Children of the Setting Sun Dance Group to Washington, D.C., to dance for the presidents and the Indian commissioners, proving to them that the Lummi culture was alive. He also took his dance group to fairs all over the United States, where he represented the Lummi tribe.

Many of the songs and dances which Pauline teaches were used by the elders to impart to the younger generations the skills needed for survival through the centuries. The song she sings here is the "Chief's Song." Many years ago, there was a song for every activity in a village. Every person had a special song of their own. The chief's song was called the *čǝlangʼan* song, in which he asks the listeners to look at the wealth of his heritage and tells them how he loves his way of life. At the end, the little children danced. Today, the song is used both as a welcoming song for dignitaries and to honor veterans on Veterans' Day. It is sung in the Lummi language.

langət ʔə tsa ⎫
aʔlo langʔət(s) siʔam ⎬ Look at the wealth of my heritage
langət ʔə tsa ⎪
aʔlo langʔət(s) siʔam ⎭

niɬnə čəlangʔan siʔam ⎫ I love my way of life
niɬnə čəlangʔan siʔam ⎭

8. Paddle Song/Welcome Song. Lillian Pullen, Quileute

Lillian Pullen is a traditional basket maker, a Quileute tribal elder, and teacher from La Push, where the tribe is based at the mouth of the Quileute River, on the Pacific coast of the Olympic Peninsula. One of the few remaining Quileute basket makers, she learned her skill from her grandmother and other elderly tribal women. From them Lillian also learned Quileute songs and dances.

Known as "Grandma Lillian," she is renowned for her efforts to preserve and pass on her people's language and culture. She helped develop the Quileute Dictionary and the Tribal School Cultural Enrichment Program. Now in her eighties, she is one of the last fluent Quileute speakers. She continues to teach the language to a new generation of children at the Tribal School. Lillian describes the Quileute language as "a custom, a tradition of our elders living here years ago. It shows the outside world we are a race of people who are proud to have our heritage."

This song comes from Lillian's grandfather, Chief Tommy Penn. He lived at *kaʔloʔiwa* (halfway between here and there). This was the homestead near the current site of Forks. The song is now used as a welcoming song to visitors to the reservation and when canoes travel to other locations. It calls peoples together. It is sung to bid them good-bye. It is sung as the canoe is paddled, both in rivers and in salt water. The text consists of vocables: the meaning of the song is in its sounds and rhythms, not its words.

9. Indian Shaker Song. Lillian Pullen, Quileute

This song is a hymn from Lillian's church, where she is an assistant minister. She says: "I'm always singing. That's what we do when we are basket-weaving. Me, anyway. The sacred songs come to me because it lifts everything from your heart, how you feel, You relax then. God's helping you. The meaning of this song is something that could never be expressed in words. It comes from the spirit. We receive it and sing it. It empowers you. It is a healing song, as is any Shaker song. When you touch people, they begin to feel better. It is sacred."

10. Seafood Song. Lillian Pullen, Quileute

The Seafood Song, given to Lillian by her grandmother, used to be sung by her to show her joy at finding the seafood. The song, however, is sung from the point of view of *claʔa čǝt* (stuck-on-the-rock), that is, a limpet.

TRANSLATION

With the help of the kelp / That is on my back / I will move from rock to rock / Until I find a space.

> ʔa la k'It t'su kʷaʔtǝs
> yǝx̌ he yʔštay ya ašʔtil
> ʔa he ʔe ya ʔe ya ʔe ya ʔa
> hʔi ʔa ʔe ʔi ya ʔa
> (repeat)
> ʔuuš (end)

Eastern Washington

11. Owl Dance Song. James Selam, Yakama

The native name of the Yakama is *waptailmim*, 'people of the narrow river' or *pa'kiut'lema* 'people of the gap.' Both names refer to the narrows in the Yakima River at Union Gap, where the tribe's chief village was formerly situated. For more information, see Chapter 6, "Song Traditions of the Yakama."

The Selam family is known among the Yakama people for its traditional ways. James Selam, who lives in Granger, retains a wide repertoire of traditional songs; he and his brother Howard have contributed much to the Yakama Nation's efforts to preserve and protect this repertoire. This selection, as well as the next, represents a social dance in 3/4 meter in which both women and men participate. James Selam is one of the last elders who knows these two traditional songs. The Owl Dance is a couples' dance that was used in courtship. Then, the young woman would have chosen her dance partner, following instructions from her parents, who would have wanted to arrange a good marriage for her. The dance, which was traditionally done at night (the owl which gives its name to the dance is nocturnal), is still performed today, but may take place in daylight. A man and a woman face each other and move in a step-slide, step-slide pattern, keeping rhythm with the drum.

TRANSLATION

Two, two, two, two (people), / step out here (to dance).
>*na pu na pu na pu na pu wiyawiyapiin* (repeat three times)
>*wi ah we*

12. Willow Song. James Selam, Yakama

James Selam has taught many people about Yakama songs, including the historically significant work songs inspired by life on the Columbia River. The Willow Dance, which is a Selam family song, is a work song. Willow branches were gathered as material to make winter lodges, and the bark was shredded and used to make rope to lace tule mats together. It is also used in making fish traps. After their work, people would gather in the evening and do the Willow Dance, holding willow, and rocking and sliding as they danced in a circle. At a certain time, when the drum was hit, all the partners switched sides and reversed direction.

13. Food Gathering Song. Jeanette Timentwa, Okanogan

Jeanette Timentwa, from the Colville Confederated Tribes in north-central Washington, is widely known for her traditional knowledge, which includes that of medicines, herbs, and foods. A number of songs in Jeanette's repertoire, such as root gathering songs, are connected with foods and medicines. Although this is a food gathering song, according to Jeanette it will help those with a drinking problem as well as inspire hunters, fishers, and berry gatherers. Songs are used as prayers and supplications to bring humility. The more downcast one feels, the more the Creator will be inclined to help one out.

She explains the importance of her Food Gathering Song: "As a little girl, I got lost for four days and four nights. [When] I got older [I knew that] I had to sing this song. That [if I did], I would never go hungry. And it's true. When I send my grandsons or anybody out hunting, they come back with plenty of deer. When I go berry picking or go root digging I always get what [food] I need for my winter dances."

14. Intertribal Powwow Song: Women's Traditional Dance.
The Rising Son Drum Group, Nez Perce (Nespelum)

The Rising Son drum group from Spokane is one of the best known intertribal groups in the state. Here they present a dance song which is performed at powwows. The inspiration for the graceful Women's Traditional Dance comes from the time

12. Performance at Northwest Folklife Festival, 1992. Bruce-*subiyay* Miller, with his sister Leona-*babʔtahl* Miller and nephew Adam-*kwa ahlkaydɔb* Visser. *Photograph by Lou Corbett*

13. Johnny Moses, Northwest Folklife Festival, 1992. *Photograph by Lou Corbett*

14. The Swan family, Northwest Folklife Festival, 1992. *Photograph by Lou Corbett*

15. Pauline Hillaire, Northwest Folklife Festival, 1992. *Photograph by Lou Corbett*

16. Lillian Pullen, Northwest Folklife Festival, 1992. *Photograph by Lou Corbett*

17. Rising Son Drum Group, Northwest Folklife Festival, 1992. *Photograph by Lou Corbett*

18. The Quileute dancers, Northwest Folklife Festival, 1992. *Photograph by Lou Corbett*

19. The Sijohn family on stage, Northwest Folklife Festival, 1992. *Photograph by Lou Corbett*

20. *Right to left:* James Selam, his son Willie, and brother Howard at the Northwest Folklife Festival, 1992. *Photograph by Lou Corbett*

21. Fred Hill Sr., with two deerskin drums that he made.
Photograph by Jens Lund; courtesy of Washington State Arts Commission

when the warriors returned from battle. The women dressed in their finest buckskin clothing and expressed their joy in a dignified manner, gracefully moving around the dance floor with precise rhythmic footwork, honoring their return.

15. Honor Song. The George Family, Yakama

The George family not only continues the old Yakama song traditions, but they have composed modern songs based on the traditional models. They are well known for winning many song and drum competitions. This rendition of the Honor Song includes both men and women singers. The participation of women around the drum is a recent innovation, for in past generations propriety dictated that women did not sing or drum in public gatherings except during serenade songs. The George family includes their daughters. Their higher-pitched voices add more alto and soprano strength to the singing.

This song, which is used all across North America, is sung to honor veterans and whenever the flag is raised. At veterans' gatherings it is sung during flag raising, early in the morning when the men come dancing out with an Indian flag. This song can also be sung to honor prominent visitors, on special occasions, for a memorial, for a chief, or for tribal elders.

Listen for a victory yell in the middle of the song.

16. Flute and Dance Song. Cliff Sijohn and the Sijohn Family, Spokane

The Sijohn family, from the Spokane Nation in eastern Washington, are well known throughout the region. They were the focus of the documentary *Circle of Song*, referred to in Chapter 3. Led by Mr. Francis Sijohn, the family has a number of excellent dancers who compete in the powwow circuits and give demonstrations at cultural events. Spokane, which means "Children of the Sun," is the name applied to several small bands of Salishan speakers who live around the Spokane River.

The Plateau courting flute, often fabricated of hollowed elderberry wood, produced pentatonic melodies unique to each instrument. Mr. Sijohn, who plays the flute prelude to the dance song, illustrates the playing style with long-held tones interspersed with quick florid ornaments which are reminiscent of coyote "yips."

17. Stick Game Song. The Sijohn and Nomee Families, Spokane

This friendly game between two families illustrates the alternating use of power songs to confuse and distract the guessing team (see number 6 above, Bone Game Song). This selection is a combination of two stick (or bone) game songs, both quite ancient. Halfway through the first song, a new song begins. It has an entirely different melody and rhythm. The transition between songs happens without any noticeable change in the intensity of the game, and occurs because the location of the sticks (game pieces) was guessed correctly by the opposing team. Since they now have the advantage, they begin a new song and the sticks are passed to them. The teams alternate songs until the game ends. The two teams are the Sijohn and Nomee families.

18. Shake Hands Song, *Kaks En-Pee-e'l-see.* Sacred Heart Mission Choir: Kalispel, Spokane, and Coeur d'Alene Catholic singers

This translated Christian hymn, "Let Us Be Happy and Sing," has become the traditional ending to Catholic masses celebrated among the interior Salish east of the Cascades. The priest and other celebrants stand in a row, shaking hands with every worshipper in passing. Each one then joins the lengthening circle until all have greeted one another.

TRANSLATION

Let us be happy, / Indeed let us sing, / God's son / Because of the pitiful Indians / From on high He has come down, / He has come down, Jesus.

> *Kaks en-pee-e'l-see*
> *Shay kaks en-ku-n'em,*
> *Ko-lin-tsu'-ten sku-se's*
> *Whel knon-quint łu sky'* [*ee-whu*]
> *Te'l en-wee'st es tswa-mist,*
> *Tswel-kup hest Yay-su.*

19. Round Dance Song. Fred Hill, Sr., Yakama/Umatilla/Nez Perce

Fred Hill, Sr., is a singer, dancer, and drum maker who lives in the little community of Georgeville, south of the Status Pass summit. Among his teachers Fred has been especially influenced by Leroy Selam and Charles McKay. Now a respected lead drummer and singer of traditional songs himself, he has been teaching Yakama songs and drum making to tribal youth for many years.

"Our roots are tied to the Columbia River or as we call it Nch'i-wana 'The Big River,'" he says. "Our customs revolve around the drum and this is the way of life for our people. There are wedding songs, laughing songs, war dance songs, owl and rabbit dance songs, and many countless more. I have been asked to teach because there are only 5 percent who speak Yakama on our reservation. Many of our elders are too old to hike the mountains and have consented for me to properly teach our young since I have the health to do so."

His first song is a Round Dance song which he learned from Bill Johnson, Sr. For it, he plays a drum especially made for Round Dance songs. Fred emphasizes the importance of learning to drum before trying to sing dance songs with drum accompaniment. By doing so, the rhythm of the song and drumbeat are tightly merged. This song has vocables.

20. Hungry Song. Fred Hill, Sr., Yakama/Umatilla/Nez Perce

This song comes from Fred Hill's Nez Perce relatives and elders. They called it "The Hungry Song."

TRANSLATION

Where can I be? Where can I be? I want bread.

21. Eagle Song. Fred Hill, Sr., Yakama/Umatilla/Nez Perce

Fred's next song is about Eagle. It is a song that came to him after much prayer and contemplation. It is in the Yakama dialect of the Sahaptin language.

TRANSLATION

The Eagle is helping us.
With these feathers, we are dancing.
Now you, my people, dance!

22. Salmon Story Song. Martin Louie, Colville Confederated Tribes

Martin Louie has long been a ceremonial leader on the Colville Reservation, and has been working hard to preserve their songs and legends. He has worked closely with youth from all the Colville nations, teaching them traditional values and cultural expressions, such as sweatlodge songs and ceremonies.

Martin has taught his two sons much of what he knows, and both speak the native Lakes language. His repertoire of traditional songs includes victory dances, burial dances, war, root, berry, salmon, hunting, sweatlodge, and game songs, learned mostly from his grandfather, whose traditional ways strongly influenced Martin as a child.

This is a story-song about Coyote and how he distributed salmon among the eastern Washington tribes, ending at Kettle Falls. He sang a variation of this song each time he gave the salmon to his people. Martin tells how the story ends:

> When he got there [Kettle Falls], he told the people, "Here's what you guys want— here's the fish. Go look in the trap." They went in. There was a male salmon and a female salmon there. He said, "All right, we'll cook that salmon. There's a kettle right on the edge of the falls. There is a hole. I saw it. It's deep."
>
> That's where they cooked the salmon. They heated rocks and put them in the water. They boiled the salmon and fed a good many hundred people. Each got a little piece. He distributed the salmon all over. Every place he stopped he said, "This is going to be the traditional song for the salmon feast."

Elaine Emerson, a Colville cultural leader and language teacher, elaborates:

> There are many versions of the salmon story. In the old days it would take many days or nights to tell one story. Often Coyote told the people that he would bring the salmon up the Columbia River and its tributaries, but only if he could have a beautiful woman for his wife.
>
> The way the song is sung suggests an image of the salmon swimming up river. There are holes in rocks at Kettle Falls. They were made by small, swirling rocks carving a hole in the other rocks.

WILLIE SMYTH is the folk arts coordinator for the Washington State Arts Commission. He has written two books and eighteen articles focusing on a wide range of cultures and traditional expressions, and coordinated musical events including "Songs of Indian Territory: Native American Music Traditions of Oklahoma," "Juneteenth on Greenwood: A Celebration of Oklahoma's Black Music Traditions," and "*Gritos del Alma*: Chicano/Mexicano Music Traditions of Washington State."

Traditional Songs

The following is a list of the songs discussed in this chapter, numbered according to track on the accompanying recording. *The songs in this collection belong to the individuals and families who shared them. To use them without the permission of these individuals or families is a violation of copyright law.*

Western Washington

1. Chinook Changer Song
    Bruce-*subiyay* Miller
2. The Thunderbird Song
    Bruce-*subiyay* Miller
3. Indian Shaker Song
    Johnny Moses
4. Baby Teasing Song
    Johnny Moses
5. T'abaa Song
    Helma Swan
6. Bone Game Song
    Helma Swan
7. Lummi Chief's Song
    Pauline Hillaire
8. Paddle Song / Welcome Song
    Lillian Pullen
9. Indian Shaker Song
    Lillian Pullen
10. Seafood Song
    Lillian Pullen

Eastern Washington

11. Owl Dance Song
    James Selam
12. Willow Song
    James Selam
13. Food Gathering Song
    Jeanette Timentwa
14. Women's Traditional Dance
    Rising Son
15. Honor Song
    The George Family
16. Flute and Dance Song
    Cliff Sijohn and the Sijohn Family
17. Stick Game Song
    The Sijohn and Nomee Families
18. Shake Hands Song
    Sacred Heart Mission Choir
19. Round Dance Song
    Fred Hill, Sr.
20. Hungry Song
    Fred Hill, Sr.
21. Eagle Song
    Fred Hill, Sr.
22. Salmon Story-Song
    Martin Louie

Appendix 1

Ten Early Ethnographers in the Northwest:

Recordings from Washington State

LAUREL SERCOMBE

A SEARCH FOR ETHNOGRAPHIC RECORDINGS OF THE MUSIC OF the indigenous people of the state of Washington might reasonably begin in the collections of the public archives, libraries, and museums of that state. Several such collections are located on the University of Washington campus in Seattle. Both the Melville Jacobs Collection in the University Libraries and the Leon Metcalf Collection in the Burke Museum are rich sources of recorded songs as well as myths, tales, and other spoken materials. The Ethnomusicology Archives, in the Ethnomusicology Division of the School of Music, also include several collections of recorded songs. However, the search for collections containing the music of Washington's First People soon leads away from the Northwest.

As with the earliest ethnographic research on the Pacific Coast, conducted in British Columbia and Alaska, early field research in Washington State was initiated and conducted by members of the fledgling discipline of anthropology, centered in New York and Chicago. With the advent of sound recording technology and its application to ethnographic fieldwork in the 1890s, wax cylinder recordings became not only a new form of documentation but also a new kind of cultural artifact. This was still the age of collecting, and cylinders containing aural specimens were carried home from the field and deposited in institutional collections for classification, duplication, and preservation. Recordings were often shelved without further study, and in many cases they are not even mentioned in the publications of the scholars who made them.

As a result of these early research methods and the development of large repositories of cylinder recordings in the Bureau of American Ethnology (now at the Smithsonian Institution) and the American Museum of Natural History, the majority of recordings made in the Northwest are located, not in the Northwest at all, but in the large archival collections at Indiana University, the Library of Congress, and the Smithsonian Institution. The objective of this appendix is to present a comprehensive list of the whereabouts of collections of ethnographic recordings produced in Washington and to provide some historical background on collections recorded between 1898 and World War II.

All the collections located were compiled by non-Native outsiders who entered Native communities for a variety of research purposes. Their recordings are located mainly in archives, but a few are in private collections. Most of these collections are listed in published catalogs, such as the Federal Cylinder Project guides published by the Library of Congress and the indexes to the collections in the Archives of Traditional Music at Indiana University. In Washington State we have two fine indexes: the *Guide to the Nez Perce Music Archive* by Loran Olsen (1989) and the *Guide to the Pacific Northwest Native American Materials in the Melville Jacobs Collection and in Other Archival Collections in the University of Washington Libraries* by William R. Seaburg (1982). These and other sources provided the information from which the accompanying list has been assembled.

Music of the First People

What do these collections contain, and what do they tell us about the musical expression of the First People of Washington? Without exception, they are collections of songs. With few exceptions, the songs are performed by one person, sometimes with accompanying voices and/or drums. The kinds of songs include personal songs, doctors' songs, game songs, love songs, war songs, secret society songs, potlatch songs, dance songs, children's songs, lullabies, gambling songs, canoe songs, shaman's songs, and myth songs. We know that singing was part of all kinds of ceremonial and social occasions, many of which continue to thrive. In the case of some songs, however, the appropriate performance setting no longer existed or had been drastically altered by the time recordings were made. The singers themselves may never have heard the songs in their historical context, or may have recalled those occasions from childhood. In all cases, the requirements of recording technology (such as placement of the recording horn, and later the microphone, or problems related to powering the recording device) resulted in the removal of the song performance from any natural context.

A second kind of "decontextualization" occurred with the recording of myth and tale songs. Story texts were generally transcribed manually, and only the songs occurring within stories were recorded with sound recording equipment. The separate recording of songs, when it occurred at all, resulted in a displacement of music from text in folklore collections. Myths, tales, and other folklore have been transcribed, studied, and published as collections of text, while integrally related song recordings have generally remained unstudied on archive shelves. As a result, our knowledge of songs and their role in indigenous folklore remains meager. Since what we do know about Native music in the state of Washington as it was practiced between 1898 and 1950 has been formed almost entirely from song recordings, we are left, at best, with an incomplete and distorted picture of musical activity.

Recorded collections notwithstanding, the music culture of the Northwest has been largely neglected by those who have studied this area over the last century. We know much more about the languages, mythology, subsistence, and arts of the First People than we do about their music. The reasons for this probably have to do not only with the limitations of recording technology and the decontextualization of song performance, but with the priorities of early ethnographers, who were in a hurry to make a record of human cultures, including languages, that they believed to be doomed to extinction. A final factor contributing to the neglect of music culture was the lack of scholars trained and committed to ethnomusicological research in the Northwest.

The fact that there exists a considerable body of recorded songs, but little in the way of study and analysis of them, was noted in 1934 by anthropologist Melville Jacobs. In the course of his extensive fieldwork in eastern Washington and western Oregon, Jacobs recorded hundreds of songs, but he believed that music should be studied by scholars trained in what we would now call ethnomusicology. He wrote:

> Since there is now perhaps no expert resident in the Northwest competent to transcribe and conduct research in Indian music, our principal interest so far has been collection rather then study. In effect we have been building an archive composed of music given by natives spontaneously during the course of our field ethnologic and folkloric researches. The purpose is to collect the music in its natural setting in the ethnologic work, and to forestall irretrievable loss and extinction if lone survivors or the few remaining remnants of a tribe die before the advent of a musicologist as such. (Seaburg 1982:39)

Jacobs's observations reflect the anthropological ideology of his time. It was considered not only the right but the duty of ethnographers of Native cultures to collect and preserve as much evidence of expressive culture—music, as well as the language and folklore—as possible. However, as Jacobs notes, the collecting of music recordings is one thing and the study of a group's music quite another.

The Collectors

Ten ethnographers conducted field research in Washington before World War II. Of these, the most influential was Franz Boas (1858–1942), one of the founders of American anthropology, who had some measure of responsibility for nearly all the anthropological, linguistic, and musical research in the Northwest from the 1890s through the 1930s. Boas was on the faculty at Columbia University from 1896 until his retirement in 1937, and six of the ten early fieldworkers in Washington were in fact his students: Livingston Farrand, Leo J. Frachtenberg, Herman K. Haeberlin, Erna Gunther, Thelma Adamson, and Melville Jacobs. Of the remaining three, the most well known are Edward S. Curtis and Frances Densmore; the third was a local collector named Arthur C. Ballard. The collectors are discussed in chronological order.

Boas himself made thirteen field trips to the Northwest (Rohner 1969:309–13), and he sent students over the course of four generations to study the Native peoples of the Northwest Coast area. Boas's own recordings of Kwakiutl (now known as the Kwakwaka'wakw) and Thompson River songs, made in 1893 or 1895, were, in fact, the first in situ recordings of Northwest Coast songs. (Songs by the Kwakiutl had previously been recorded at the World's Columbian Exposition in Chicago in 1893.) Boas also published over a hundred musical transcriptions during the course of his career (Ellingson 1992:118). He felt strongly that songs should be recorded whenever possible for later analysis by trained music scholars, and he encouraged all his students to record songs in the course of their fieldwork.

The first Washington voices heard on cylinder recordings were those of a Quileute woman (whose English name was Eunice) and four Quinaults (identified as Liza, Jesse, Lucy, and Jim Cape). All were recorded in 1898 by Livingston Farrand (1867–1939), who visited the coast of Washington that year and again in 1900 as part of the Jesup North Pacific Expedition, directed by Boas. The songs Farrand recorded are not mentioned in his collection of Quinault tales, and we know nothing about his consultants other than their English first names. The recordings are located at Indiana University.

The next recordings in the state were made by Edward S. Curtis (1868–1952), famous for his portrait photographs of North American Indians. In addition to producing more than 40,000 photographs and several films, he is estimated to have overseen the recording of several thousand cylinders. The whereabouts of many of these cylinder recordings are not known, but 279 of the total, recorded between 1907 and 1913, are at Indiana University. They represent numerous North American groups, including songs from several in Washington State identified as Klikitat, Wishram, Yakama, Makah, Snohomish (uncertain), and other unidentified groups (Seeger and Spear 1987:80–83).

Curtis was not a trained anthropologist, and Franz Boas resented his work and its unscholarly, sometimes sensationalistic character. This resentment probably stemmed in part from territoriality. Not only did ethnographers of this early period believe they had the right to appropriate any and all items of interest to them from Native communities, but they actually claimed geographical areas, and their inhabitants, as their own research "territory." Boas explicitly claimed the Northwest Coast as his own, and he made it clear that he considered it a matter of honor that other scholars respect those boundaries.

Leo J. Frachtenberg (1883–1930) and Herman K. Haeberlin (1892–1918) were Boas's students. Both were in the field in 1916 and 1917, Frachtenberg in La Push and Haeberlin in the "Puget Sound District" working with the Snohomish and Snoqualmie. Frachtenberg recorded eighty-two cylinders of songs by ten Quileute consultants, now at the Library of Congress (Gray 1988:223). Haeberlin's recordings were the first in the Northwest to be used as Boas had envisioned. Helen Roberts, another student of Boas, who had studied music at the American Conservatory of Music, transcribed and analyzed the recordings and collaborated with Haeberlin on an article entitled "Some Songs of the Puget Sound Salish" (Roberts and Haeberlin 1918). The article named the local consultants and provided information about the sources of eleven songs and the occasions for their use. Also provided are musical scores of ten of the songs with original texts (or nonlexical vocables), each accompanied by text translations and Roberts's musical analysis. The Haeberlin recordings are now housed at Indiana University. After his death, Haeberlin's research notes on the Puget Sound Salish were transferred by Boas to Erna Gunther (Amoss 1988:134), who published *The Indians of Puget Sound* under both their names, first in German in 1924 and then in English (Haeberlin and Gunther 1930). She also edited Haeberlin's *Mythology of Puget Sound* (Haeberlin 1924).

Frances Densmore (1867–1957), a prolific collector of North American Indian songs for over half a century, spent only a brief time in the Northwest. In 1923 and

1926 she visited Neah Bay on the Makah Reservation and recorded Clayoquot, Makah, and Quileute songs. She also recorded one cylinder of Yakama material in 1926 in Chilliwack, British Columbia. These recordings are at the Library of Congress (Gray 1988). Densmore published a monograph on her Northwest work, *Nootka and Quileute Music* (1939).

Densmore has a unique place in the history of Native American music research. Trained in music, not anthropology, she worked during the age of Boas but mainly outside his sphere of influence. Her work was conducted for many years under the auspices of the Bureau of American Ethnology, which sponsored her field research and published her monographs. Her expertise in the collection, description, and analysis of Native American music was acknowledged by the founders of the formal discipline of ethnomusicology in the early 1950s (Frisbie 1991). (See Gray's appendix in this volume for more information about Densmore's work.)

Erna Gunther (1896–1982) was best known in the state of Washington as the director of the Washington State Museum (now the Burke Museum of Natural History and Culture), a position she held for over thirty years. A student of Boas, Gunther first came to Seattle in 1921 and completed her doctorate from Columbia in 1928. She subsequently became the executive officer of the University of Washington's Anthropology Department. Her earliest recordings are cylinder recordings of songs by Joe Johnson and Robert Collier of the Klallam people, recorded in Jamestown, Washington, in 1925 and now in the collection at Indiana University. Neither of her two publications on the Klallam, *Klallam Folk Tales* (1925) and *Klallam Ethnography* (1927), mentions these songs. The guide to the Jacobs Collection also lists three aluminum disc recordings Gunther made in 1935 containing Makah and Quinault language (although perhaps no songs). These recordings were assigned numbers by Jacobs, but their location is not currently known (Seaburg 1982:76).

Thelma Adamson (1901–83) and Melville Jacobs (1902–71) were classmates who studied with Boas at Columbia University in the mid-1920s. They both did fieldwork in the Northwest during the summers of 1926 and 1927. During the second summer, they were joined by Boas himself and a cylinder recorder. Three collections of recordings were made during the summer of 1927, including songs by Upper Chehalis, Cowlitz, Klikitat, and Yakama consultants. The cylinders were taken east and deposited at the American Museum of Natural History in New York; they are now housed at Indiana University (Seeger and Spear 1987).

Adamson and Jacobs both obtained positions at the University of Washington in 1928, and Boas must have felt that his Northwest outpost was secured. He viewed the two as his resident fieldworkers. Jacobs, at least, was committed to recording music in the course of his linguistic research; he hoped that his music recordings would be transcribed and analyzed by George Herzog, another Boas student and a scholar of what was then called comparative musicology. (See Seaburg appendix in this volume.) Adamson did not stay at the University of Washington; in fact, by the time her *Folk-Tales of the Coast Salish* was published along with song transcriptions by Herzog (1934), illness had already ended her career in anthropology. Jacobs, on the other hand, was to stay at the University of Washington until his death in 1971—teaching, conducting research in Washington and Oregon, and building his collection of recordings, both his own and those of other collectors. The collaborative projects he envisioned with Herzog to study the songs in Jacobs's collection never materialized, however. Among Jacobs's students who recorded and studied music of the Northwest in the 1950s and 1960s were Paul Fetzer, Virginia Mohling, and Vivian Williams, whose collections appear on the accompanying list. The Jacobs Collection includes numerous recordings made in Washington State, including Upper Cowlitz, Klikitat, Yakama, Muckleshoot, Duwamish, Lummi, Twana, Nooksack, Puyallup, Makah, Snohomish, Swinomish, Skagit, Quileute, and Quinault consultants.

The last of the prewar collectors to make cylinder recordings was Arthur C. Ballard (1876–1962), a businessman from Auburn, Washington, with a personal interest in the preservation of Native culture. Working independently, he began collecting Southern Lushootseed myths from Snoqualmie, Puyallup, and Duwamish speakers in 1916. In 1929, the University of Washington Press published his *Mythology of Southern Puget Sound,* a collection of 126 stories (including multiple versions) by twenty-seven consultants (Ballard 1929). Ballard provided the names of his consultants, as well as those of their parents and grandparents and additional genealogical information, in unusual detail for the time. Ballard collected these stories mainly in their original language, but published only the English translations. The song texts within the stories, however, are given in the original language. In 1932, Ballard made Ediphone cylinder recordings of four of his consultants singing twelve Puget Sound Salish songs, eleven of which correspond to myth songs in the published collection. These recordings are in the Jacobs Collection at the University of Washington.

The control Boas maintained over fieldwork activities in the Northwest during this period may be illustrated by an excerpt from a letter written by Boas to Ballard in 1928, the year Melville Jacobs and Thelma Adamson arrived at the University of Washington. Boas had been made aware of Ballard's work in a letter from Leslie Spier, member of the University of Washington's anthropology faculty and Erna Gunther's husband, who apparently had suggested that some funds might be found to assist Ballard in his fieldwork. Boas writes:

You may know that two of my students have been appointed at the University of Washington particularly for the purpose of continuing field work and I feel quite certain that they will be glad to cooperate with you.

If you have the opportunity I wish you would be good enough to discuss any work that you yourself would like to do with them and it is not impossible that perhaps a little money might be found to pay for expenses connected with investigations. (Boas 1972: reel 29; Boas to Ballard 1/27/28)

The same day, Boas wrote to Jacobs regarding Ballard: "You will have to judge yourself whether it seems profitable to cooperate with him. I presume the sum referred to by Spier might perhaps be found" (Boas 1972: reel 29; Boas to Jacobs 1/27/28).

The last prewar sound recordings made in Washington are Duwamish myth dictations by Julia Siddle, recorded by Jacobs in 1936. In 1933 Jacobs had obtained funding for the construction of a portable electric phonograph recorder; beginning in July 1934, all his field recordings were produced with this equipment. This change in technology for Jacobs corresponds roughly with the end of the early ethnographic collecting era and the widespread transition to field recordings made on acetate and aluminum discs. A small corpus of disc recordings was produced in western Washington during the 1940s, including the Lummi, Lower Chehalis, and Duwamish recordings of John Paul Marr (as part of the research endeavors of John P. Harrington) in 1941 and the Twana songs recorded by William Elmendorf in 1946. Also during this period, a field survey was in progress to record and publish music from Native American communities around the United States. Willard Rhodes, a professor of music at Columbia University, conducted nine surveys between 1940 and 1952, visiting the Puget Sound region in 1950 to record songs of a number of local groups, including examples in Chinook Jargon and Indian Shaker Church songs. In 1954, the Library of Congress issued ten volumes of "Music of the American Indian" on long-playing records to distribute to Indian schools and agencies and to make available for sale to the general public. Nineteen of the songs recorded in western Washington in 1950 are included on the volume "Northwest (Puget Sound)" (Library of Congress AFS L34), which is still available on cassette. The complete collection of Rhodes's field recordings is in the UCLA Ethnomusicology Archive, with duplicates at the Library of Congress.

With the advent of consumer analog tape recording technology around 1950, ethnographic field recording ceased to be the domain of the institutionally supported academic researcher. One private collector in Washington State, Leon Metcalf, deserves special mention here because of the size and richness of his collection and its importance as a local resource. Metcalf grew up in the Northwest in the early 1900s, was trained in music, and had a long career in music education. He had known Native people as a child and developed a lifelong interest in the languages of the Northwest. In 1950 he acquired a tape recorder and began meeting and recording Native speakers. At the urging of Martin Sampson, a Swinomish-Skagit culture bearer and the son of Upper Skagit historian Susie Sampson Peter, Metcalf concentrated on the collection of myths. Between 1950 and 1961 he recorded seventy-five reels of Northwest Native speech and music, seventy-three of which are from within Washington. Of those seventy-three reels, sixteen contain songs. As mentioned above, the Metcalf collection is one of the two largest collections recorded in the state of Washington still located here.

A list of other collections with interesting stories behind them follows this article. Perhaps the most interesting stories are those we know least about—the stories of the men and women who spoke the myths and tales and sang the songs of their people into the recording horns and microphones. We know them only through their voices, which for nearly one hundred years have been preserved on cylinder, disc, wire, and tape. These ethnographic recordings remain a unique document of the culture of Washington's First People.

LAUREL SERCOMBE is the archivist for the University of Washington Ethnomusicology Archives, a position she has held since 1982. She has a B.A. in music and a master of librarianship degree and is currently a candidate for her doctorate in ethnomusicology, with a specialty in historical recordings of Lushootseed songs.

Key to List of Ethnographic Recordings

The accompanying list presents data about recordings chronologically by year of recording. For each collection the following information is provided (when known):

Name(s) of collectors/researchers

Year(s) of recording

Song types (these have been compiled from indexes to the various collections and may not be consistent or complete)

Name of group recorded

Name(s) of singers/consultants

Location where recordings were made

Current location of the collection:

1. Indiana University Archives of Traditional Music (Bloomington)
2. Library of Congress Archive of Folk Culture, American Folklife Center (Washington, D.C.)
3. University of Washington Libraries (Seattle)
4. Burke Museum, University of Washington (Seattle)
5. University of Washington Ethnomusicology Archives (Seattle)
6. National Anthropological Archives (Washington, D.C.)
7. UCLA Ethnomusicology Archive (Los Angeles)
8. Collector

Ethnographic Recordings

Collector	Year	Song Type/ (Group)	Consultants/ (Rec. Location)	Current Location
Farrand	1898	?/(Quileute)	Eunice/ (Pt. Grenville?)	1
—	1898	?/(Quinault)	Liza, Jesse, Lucy, Jim Cape/(Pt. Grenville?)	1

Collector	Year	Song Type/ (Group)	Consultants/ (Rec. Location)	Current Location
Curtis	1907–13	Love, medicine, traveling, war/(Snohomish?)	?/(Nespelem)	1
—	1907–13	Nature/(?)	?/(Nespelem)	1
—	1907–13	Canoe, courtship, dance, lodge, love, medicine, songs for the dead, victory/(Wishram?)	?/(Wishram?)	1
—	1907–13	Whaling/(Makah)	?/(?)	1
—	1909	Dance, gambling, medicine/ (Klikitat)	?/(Klikitat)	1
—	1909	Dance, healing, love, medicine/(Yakama)	?/(Yakama Res.)	1
Haeberlin	1916	Love/(Snoqualmie)	?/(Puget Sound Dist.)	1
—	1916	Love, tribal, spirit, medicine, gambling, women's/ (Snohomish)	?/(Puget Sound Dist.)	1
Frachtenberg	1916–17	Beggar, gambling, Kiya'a, Lokwali, love, lullaby, Qel!a'akwal, Shaker, Shaman, Sibaxulayo', Tcalalayo', Ts!asa'a, Ts!ayeq, war/(Quileute)	Mr. & Mrs. Webb Jones, Old Taylor, Mrs. Johnson, Billie Hebalakup, Abeti, Talicas Eastman, Julia Lee, Mrs. Ward, Bessie Gray, Arthur Howeattle/(La Push)	2
Densmore	1923, 1926	Children's, dance, dream, feast, honoring dead, social, treating sick, war, wedding, whaling, women's/(Clayoquot)	Mrs. Sarah Guy, Annie Long Tom/(Neah Bay, Makah Res.)	2

Collector	Year	Song Type/ (Group)	Consultants/ (Rec. Location)	Current Location
—	1923, 1926	Children's, contest, dance, dream, game, healing, Klokali, legend, Makah Day, potlatch, social, social dance, war, women's, young men's/(Makah)	Young Doctor, Mrs. Wilson Parker, James Guy, etc./ (Neah Bay, Makah Res.)	2
Gunther	1925	Canoe, dance, gambling, love, puberty rites, society, spirit, thunder, war, unknown subjects/(Klallam)	Joe Johnson, Robert Collier/ (Jamestown)	1
Densmore	1926	Dance, doctoring, animal, etc./(Quileute)	Mrs. Gilbert Holden/ (Neah Bay, Makah Res.)	2
—	1926	?/(Quileute)	?/(?)	2
—	1926	?/(Yakama)	Francis James/ (Chilliwack, B.C.)	2
Adamson	1927	Children's, doctors', game, love, lullaby, mythology, snake, spirit, war, unknown subjects/ (Chehalis)	Mr. & Mrs. Dan Secena, Marion Davis, Jonas Xwan/ (Oakville)	1
Adamson & Boas	1927	Bears, chief's, deer, doctors', gambling, love, moon, shaman's and spirit, chants, lullabies, marriage rites, mythology, stories, unknown/(Chehalis)	Marion Davis/ (Oakville)	1
—	1927	Chants, gambling, myth/ (Nisqually)	Marion Davis/ (Oakville)	1

Collector	Year	Song Type/ (Group)	Consultants/ (Rec. Location)	Current Location
Jacobs	1927	Gambling, humorous, love, meeting, myth, personal/ (Cowlitz)	Mrs. Sam Eyley/ (Nesika)	1
—	1927	Gathering, humorous, lullabies, meeting, personal, work/ (Taidnapam)	Mrs. Sam Eyley/ (Nesika)	1
—	1927	Dance, feast, gathering, humorous, love, myth, personal/(Klikitat)	Mrs. Mary Hunt or Joe Hunt(?)/ (Nesika)	1
—	1927	Love/(Chinook)	Mrs. Mary Hunt or Joe Hunt(?)/ (Nesika)	1
—	1927	War/(Yakama)	Mrs. Mary Hunt or Joe Hunt(?)/ (Nesika)	1
—	1927	Gambling, war/(Yakama)	Sam Eyley/(Nesika)	1
—	1927	Medicine, meeting/ (Taidnapam)	Sam Eyley/(Nesika)	1
—	1928	?/(Upper Cowlitz)	Jim Yoke/(Lewis)	3
—	1929	Spirit power, women's, myth, fun-play/ (Klikitat)	Joe Hunt, Mary Mundi Hunt/ (Husum)	3
—	1929	Spirit power song/(Yakama)	Joe Hunt/(Husum)	3
Jacobs & Gunther	1930	?/(Muckleshoot)	Jenny Davis, Mrs. Siddell and ?/(Auburn)	3
—	1930	Love/(Duwamish)	Jenny Davis, Mrs. Siddell and ?/(Auburn)	3

Collector	Year	Song Type/ (Group)	Consultants/ (Rec. Location)	Current Location
Adamson	1932	?/(Nooksack)	?/(?)	1
Ballard	1932	Myth, love, power, medicine, shaman's, game, etc./(Snoqualmie)	Jack Stillman, Lucy Bill, Mary Jerry/(Auburn)	3
—	1932	Myth, stick game, power, etc./(Puyallup)	George Young/ (Auburn)	3
—	1932	Myth, lullaby, power, shaman's, food getting, medicine, etc./ (Duwamish)	Mary Jerry, Jack Stillman, George Young/(Auburn)	3
Gunther	1935	?/(Makah)	?/(?)	?
—	1935	?/(Quinault)	?/(?)	?
Jacobs	1936	Myths/(Duwamish)	Julia Siddle/(Seattle)	3
Harrington & Marr	1941	Dance, etc./(Lummi)	Chief Patrick George/ (Bellingham)	6
—	1941	Gambling, etc./ (Lower Chehalis)	Emma Luscier/ (Bay Center)	6
—	1941	Gambling, love, etc./ (Nisqually)	George Sandos, Andrew Sandos and unidentified singers/(?)	6
—	1941	Myth, traveler's, etc./ (Duwamish)	Peter James/(?)	6
Smith, H.	1942–43	Myth, canoe, spirit dance, disc game, chants, smokehouse speech/ (Lummi)	Julius Charles/ (Bellingham)	3
—	1942–43	Myth/(Swinomish)	Amelia Billy/ (Bellingham)	3
—	1942–43	Canoe, spirit dance, myth/(Samish)	John Lions, Mrs. John Lions/(Bellingham)	3

Collector	Year	Song Type/ (Group)	Consultants/ (Rec. Location)	Current Location
Elmendorf	1946	Spirit power, love, secret society, lullabies, ceremonial landing, drinking, myth/(Twana)	Henry Allen and ?/ (Skokomish)	3
Rhodes	1947	?/(misc.)	?/(Toppenish)	2
Fetzer	1950	?/(Nooksack)	George Swanaset, Mrs. Lotte Tom/ (Everson)	3
—	1950	?/(Halkomelem)	Mrs. Lotte Tom/ (Everson)	3
—	1950	?/(Skagit)	Mr. & Mrs. (Louisa) Charlie Anderson, Mrs. Lotte Tom/ (Everson)	3
—	1950	?/(Snoqualmie)	Mr. & Mrs. (Louisa) Charlie Anderson/ (Everson)	3
—	1950	?/(misc.)	Thomas Cline, Mrs. Louis George, Agnes James, Mrs. Lotte Tom/ (Everson)	3
Rhodes	1950	Bone game, guardian spirit, canoe, love, farewell, potlatch, story, dance, welcome, chief's/ (Lummi)	George Young, Joseph Hillaire/ (Auburn, Marietta)	7, 2
—	1950	Myth, game/(Nisqually)	George Young, Henry Allen/(Auburn, Union)	7, 2

Collector	Year	Song Type/ (Group)	Consultants/ (Rec. Location)	Current Location
Rhodes	1950	Children's story, bone game, Shaker, guardian spirit, medicine, rabbit, story, love/(Puyallup)	George Young, John Hawk, Henry Allen/ (Auburn, Union)	7, 2
—	1950	Guardian spirit, love, bone game, potlatch, gambling, Shaker/(Skokomish)	John Hawk, Jerry Meeker/ (Shelton)	7, 2
—	1950	Love, guardian spirit, marriage, Shaker, hymn/ (Snohomish)	William Gus, Mrs. William Gus, Joseph Hillaire/ (Auburn)	7, 2
—	1950	Hunting, love, guardian spirit, lullaby/ (Snoqualmie)	Betsy Lozier/ (Auburn)	7, 2
—	1950	Power, medicine/ (Nooksack)	Charles Anderson/ (Everson)	7, 2
—	1950	Power, story, animal, medicine, play, love, bone game, canoe, hymn, guardian spirit, chief's/(Skagit)	Charles Anderson, Tommy Bob, Mrs. Tommy Bob/ (Marietta, Everson)	7, 2
—	1950	Guardian spirit/(Samish)	Tommy Bob, Mrs. Tommy Bob/ (La Conner)	7, 2
—	1950	Chief's/(Swinomish)	Tommy Bob, Mrs. Tommy Bob/ (La Conner)	7, 2

Collector	Year	Song Type/ (Group)	Consultants/ (Rec. Location)	Current Location
Rhodes	1950	Shaker/(?)	Tommy Bob, Mrs. Tommy Bob, Mrs. Amelia Dan, Mrs. Amelia Billie, Harry Moses, Jessie H. Moses, Mrs. Hannah Bowechop, Mrs. Lyda Hottowe/ (La Conner, Neah Bay)	7, 2
—	1950	Guardian spirit, dance/(Clayoquot)	Mrs. Maggie Alderson, Randolph Parker, Alec Green, Mr. & Mrs. Charles Swan, Mrs. Lyda Hottowe/ (Neah Bay)	7, 2
—	1950	Love, Tsaiak, slave, wealth power, secret society, whisky/(Klallam)	Mrs. Nellie Wilkie, George Hottowe, Mrs. Lyda Hottowe, Henry Allen/ (Neah Bay, Union)	7, 2
—	1950	"Hamits," lullabies, dance, bone game, canoe, guardian spirit/(Makah)	Mrs. Lyda Hottowe, Mr. & Mrs. Charles Swan, Maggie Alderson, Randolph Parker, Alec Green, George Hottowe, Patrick Wilkie, Mrs. Nellie Wilkie/ (Neah Bay)	7, 2

Collector	Year	Song Type/ (Group)	Consultants/ (Rec. Location)	Current Location
Rhodes	1950	Potlatch, lullaby/(Nitinat)	Charles Jones-Family, Helen Peterson/ (Neah Bay)	7, 2
—	1950	Shaker, lullaby, love/ (Quinault)	Mrs. Hannah Bowechop/ (Neah Bay)	7, 2
—	1950	Chinook (Jargon) words to white tune, hymns/(?)	Stanley Gray, Henry Allen/ (La Push, Union)	7, 2
—	1950	Klukwali dance, dance, doctor's, canoe, animal, whaling, medicine man's, love/(Quileute)	Stanley Gray/ (La Push)	7, 2
—	1950	Guardian spirit/(Chehalis)	Henry Allen/(Union)	7, 2
—	1950	Love, guardian spirit, shaman power, soul recovery, lullabies, story/ (Twana)	Henry Allen/(Union)	7, 2
Metcalf	1950–61	Slahal, gambling, basket, love, spirit, war, doctoring, wolf, etc./ (Skagit)	Susie Sampson Peter, Ruth Shelton, Martin Sampson, Alfonso Sampson/ (Tulalip, Swinomish)	4
—	1951	?/(?)	William Gus, Betsy Lozier, Annie Daniels/(?)	4
—	1951	?/(Quileute)	Hal George/(?)	4
—	1951	?/(Makah)	Hal George/(?)	4

Collector	Year	Song Type/ (Group)	Consultants/ (Rec. Location)	Current Location
Smith, M., Herzog, Jacobs	1951	Gambling, myth, text/ (Puyallup)	Jerry Meeker/ (Tacoma)	3
Metcalf	1951–52	?/(Twana)	Mrs. Purdy, Grandpa Purdy/(Swinomish)	4
Herzog	1952	Music or text?/(Makah)	?/(Seattle)	3
Metcalf	1952	Nature/(Spokane)	Ella McCarty, Mattie Silas, Ellen Big Sam/(?)	4
—	1952–53	Love, Shaker, spirit, wolf/(Snohomish)	Ernest Cladosby, Martha McDewitt, Agnes James, Levi Lamont, Martha Lamont, Edward Sam/(?)	4
—	1952–53	?/(Lummi)	Agnes Cagey, Joseph Hillaire/(?)	4
—	1953	Owl dance, powwow/ (Yakama)	?/(Toppenish)	4
Prose	1953	Lullaby, doctors' songs, love song/(Quileute)	Jack Ward, Mary Ward/(La Push)	5
Tweddell	1953	Music or text?/(Snohomish)	?/(?)	3
Mohling	1955	Spirit power, soul recovery, wealth power, game, pastime-party, etc./ (Twana)	Henry Allen/(?)	?
—	1956	?/(Swinomish)	Charlie Anderson(?)/ (Everson?)	3
—	1956	?/(Skagit)	Charlie Anderson/ (Everson)	3

Collector	Year	Song Type/ (Group)	Consultants/ (Rec. Location)	Current Location
Williams	1963	Shaker, spirit, gambling, curing, war, story, etc./ (Swinomish)	Martin J. Sampson/ (Tacoma)	5
—	1963	Shaker, spirit, gambling, curing, war, story, etc./ (Skagit)	Martin J. Sampson/ (Tacoma)	5
Hess	1963	Love, myth, spirit power/ (Snohomish)	Edward H. (Hagan) Sam/(?)	5
—	1963	Warrior/(Snohomish)	Harriet Dover/(?)	5
—	1963	Spirit/(Klallam)	Harriet Dover/(?)	5
—	1963, 1966	Love, myth, warrior/ (Snohomish)	Martha Lamont/(?)	5
—	1963, 1969(?)	Spirit, power, etc./ (Snohomish)	Levi Lamont/(?)	5
—	1968	Love/(Puyallup)	Fourence Sigo/(?)	5
UW Ethno-musicology Archives	1968	Part of Seattle War Dance festival/(Yakama)	Columbia River Bend Drum Club, Women's dance group/(Alki Beach, Seattle)	5
—	1968	Part of Seattle War Dance festival/(Nez Perce)	Women's drumming and singing group/ (Alki Beach, Seattle)	5
—	1968	Part of Seattle War Dance festival/(Colville)	Women's dance group/ (Alki Beach, Seattle)	5
Rutherford	1973	Bone game songs/ (Swinomish)	Moris Dan, Mrs. Dan, grandson Henry/ (Fidalgo Island)	5
Hess	1973, 1976	?/(Skagit)	Martin J. Sampson/(?)	5

Collector	Year	Song Type/ (Group)	Consultants/ (Rec. Location)	Current Location
Goodman	1974–75	Women's dance, group dance, love, Tla'iihl, chief's, whale, Klukwali/ (Makah)	Helma Swan/ (Neah Bay)	8
Gellatly	?	Religious, sacred, medicine/ (Yakama)	Betsy Lozier/(?)	3
—	?	?/(Puyallup)	Betsy Lozier/(?)	3
—	?	Love, etc./(Snoqualmie)	Betsy Lozier/(?)	3
Hess	?	Love/(Halkomelem)	Levi Lamont/(?)	5
Singh	?	Music or text?/(Quinault)	?/(?)	3
—	?	Music or text?/(Quileute)	?/(?)	3
Unknown	?	?/(Makah)	?/(?)	3
—	?	?/(Quileute)	?/(?)	3
—	?	Dances/(?)	?/(?)	3
Swadesh	Pre-1950	Stories (songs included?)/ (Nootka)	?/(?)	2
—	Pre-1950	Stories (songs included?)/ (Makah)	?/(?)	2

Appendix 2

Creating and Disseminating Ethnographic Recordings:

Washington State Materials in Washington, D.C.

JUDITH A. GRAY

ALTHOUGH RELATIONS BETWEEN FEDERAL AGENCIES AND NATIVE American communities have rarely been smooth, the federal government has been a major institution documenting and serving as repository for cultural information.

Federal interest in documenting the cultures of Native people began in the early days of the republic. Indian agents, traders, military men, geological surveyors, and missionaries were sent questionnaires concerning the Indian people with whom they came in contact. The questions asked about numbers of people and available weaponry (for obvious political and military reasons), but also dealt with cultural matters—language structure, beliefs, foodways, and so on. This interest in gathering information was institutionalized in 1879, when the Bureau of Ethnology (later the Bureau of American Ethnology, usually known as the BAE) was established within the Smithsonian Institution to conduct "ethnographic researches among the North American Indians" (John Wesley Powell, cited in Judd 1967). Information and material objects flowed back to Washington, D.C., to be added to the collections of the national museum and archives.

In 1907, Frances Densmore of Red Wing, Minnesota, approached the BAE, asking for support in collecting Indian music. The agency agreed, making this the first time in its twenty-nine-year history that it focused directly on song traditions. Many ethnographic collectors had used the phonograph to document songs, but this tended

169

to be incidental to their main activities, such as gathering linguistic information, oral traditions, or material items. Although some collectors realized the importance of songs and would transcribe the texts and note the performance context, they still felt unable to handle this material, thinking that only a musician could cope with song analysis. Consequently, they recorded the songs on cylinders without any intention of processing the materials themselves.[1] It took Densmore, a trained musician, to propose a project specifically focused on songs. She became the most prolific collector of Native American recordings on wax cylinders, and was still carrying on fieldwork in 1954 at age eighty-seven.

After initial work in Chippewa communities in her home state of Minnesota, Densmore traveled around the United States and, on one occasion, into Canada, to collect recordings from different tribes in order to compare their song styles. She visited Washington State twice. On June 22, 1923, she decided "to go to Seattle soon" (Densmore n.d.). Within three weeks (July 9) she and her sister Margaret were on their way, arriving in Neah Bay at seven o'clock in the evening on the seventeenth after a twenty-two-hour boat trip from Seattle. On July 18 she began work at the house of her interpreter, Mrs. Hazel Parker Butler. But her sister fell ill, and they left for Seattle on July 31.

Densmore returned to Neah Bay three years later, setting up her cylinder recorder this time in the schoolroom on July 30. She stayed for a month, also recording in Young Doctor's store on August 23 and observing the first Makah Day celebration on August 26.[2] All told, she recorded 153 Makah, 51 Clayoquot, and 11 Quileute cylinders (approximately 9 1/4 hours). It was not until 1939 that her comparison of these "songs of the sea" with "Indian songs from prairie, woodland, high plateau, and desert" was published under the title *Nootka and Quileute Music* (Densmore 1939:v).

Densmore's book provides photographs and tells us a bit about the people whose songs she recorded. The Makah songs were sung by Young Doctor, Mr. and Mrs. Wilson Parker, James Guy, Helen Irving, Charles Swan, Philip Ladder, Edwin Hayte, and Chester Wandahart. The Clayoquot songs were sung by Sarah Guy and Annie Long Tom, Clayoquot women who were born on Vancouver Island, married Makah men, and moved to Neah Bay as young women. Densmore obtained the Quileute songs from Mrs. Gilbert Holden, identified as "one of the leading singers in her tribe" (Densmore 1939:xxvi), on the occasion of Mrs. Holden's visit to Neah Bay for the Makah Day celebration in August 1926. Densmore also listed a few songs attributed to undesignated Vancouver Island communities and one each for Nootka, Quinault, and Yakama; these songs are performed by some of the singers named above.[3]

Densmore, like some of her contemporaries, had a rather "hit-and-run" approach to fieldwork. Her trips were usually of short duration; she did not live with the people whose music she was studying; and she was totally dependent on translators. While at a site, she usually assigned consecutive field numbers or performer numbers to the cylinders; sometimes these were announced on the recordings themselves, elsewhere written on the storage boxes. Afterward, she typically returned to her Minnesota home, where she reorganized and transcribed the recordings she had gathered. The organizational scheme she imposed during this process (at home alone, without benefit of consultation) sometimes reflected tribal song categories, such as the Winter Ceremonial songs or the songs set apart for the Makah Day celebration described in her Northwest Coast book. But she also used categories that were probably her own generalizations rather than those of the people who sang for her—categories such as "songs connected with legends," "songs with legends told to children," "songs received in dreams by men," "songs received in dreams by women," and "social gatherings."

Although interested in general song styles, Densmore did not usually analyze song variations. She would compare repetitions or versions of a song and, to use her term, "discard" all but the "best and clearest rendition" (Densmore 1941:542). Her custom was to turn over to the Bureau those recordings that had been transcribed and to retain the rest for reuse, having dismissed them as "being near-duplicates, duplicates, or discards" (Densmore 1940).

Eventually Densmore was also hired to catalog other cylinder collections created by Bureau workers. She looked at, but was unable to catalog, the Quileute material assembled by Leo Joachim Frachtenberg (1883–1930). Frachtenberg had worked at La Push in 1915 and 1916. Toward the end of that time, it became apparent that the funds appropriated by the BAE for his work were running out. Frachtenberg's mentor, Franz Boas, arranged for additional funds from Columbia University so that Frachtenberg could complete his fieldwork. The BAE "accepted this offer, with the understanding that Dr. Frachtenberg would devote this sum to a comprehensive study of the music of the Quileute Indians, with special reference to the problem of song-variation. . . . [Dr. Frachtenberg] expects to collect about eighty songs, taking down the tune, burden, and translation of each song and obtaining the identical songs at separate times by the same and by distinct individuals" (Smithsonian 1917:117).

On a single cylinder, for example, Frachtenberg would record a particular song as sung by three or four individuals, or texted and untexted versions of the same song by the same singer. While the collection of song variants was already a matter of great interest in European and American ballad and folk song studies (see, for example, the exactly contemporaneous collection of Appalachian folk songs by Cecil Sharp, gathered between 1916–18, or his larger compilation of English songs and variants assembled between 1903 and 1923), this was perhaps the first time anyone chose to treat tribal songs as having the same potential to contribute to an understanding of the way the human mind processes the boundaries of sameness and difference. Although Frachtenberg himself did not undertake the detailed melodic and textual analysis characteristic of studies that try to determine how much a given song can vary and still be recognized within the culture as the same song, the way in which he made these recordings set the stage for similar research.

Frachtenberg collected at least eighty-two cylinders and mailed them off to the BAE on January 6, 1917. But he did not send along his documentation of the recordings, and this was the reason Densmore could not catalog them. Neither Frachtenberg and his contemporaries nor the institutions that became the repositories of their collections generally thought in terms of multiformat collections. Materials were often separated according to medium: recordings went one place, photographs to another, manuscripts yet elsewhere. While this makes some archival sense, due to the specialized care needed for each kind of material, it complicates the task of anyone seeking to learn how a particular ethnographer documented cultural traditions, or how a particular collection came to be.

In this case, Frachtenberg's field notes, including two notebooks labeled "Quileute songs," were eventually deposited in the American Philosophical Society Library in Philadelphia. Franz Boas's papers, also at that institution, include letters from Frachtenberg that list, among other things, the amounts he paid each singer, ranging from sixty cents each to Bessie Gray and Julia Lee to $3.30 for Webb Jones. (The interpreter, Arthur Howeattle, was paid $8.70 for his services.) Other singers were Abeti, Talicas Eastman, Billie Hebalakup, Mrs. Webb Jones, Mrs. Johnson, Old Taylor, and Mrs. S. Ward. (To place the fees in perspective, note that Frachtenberg paid $5.00 for two cords of wood, $11.50 for a total of nine lunches in Portland, $2.50 for the train from Portland to Spokane, and $3.30 per night for his hotel in Spokane.) Photocopies of some of this information are now available to those who listen to the recordings in the Folklife Reading Room at the Library of Congress.

The Densmore and Frachtenberg collections are the only cylinder-based recordings from Washington State in the Library of Congress. For specific information on the contents of the Densmore and Frachtenberg cylinder collections, see the entries in the Northwest Coast/Arctic section in volume 3 of *The Federal Cylinder Project: A Guide to Field Cylinder Collections in Federal Agencies*.

The Library's Archive of Folk Culture also contains five wire recordings of Makah and Nootka stories, speeches, and songs gathered by Morris Swadesh. Originally deposited in the American Philosophical Society Library, the 2 1/2 hours of recordings came to the Library of Congress accompanied by little documentation. One performer is referred to as "Old Galleck"; the others are unidentified. One of the spools was clearly recorded at some community event, but the place and date are not given. It is unclear whether these recordings are all from Washington State. Those wishing copies of the material need to obtain permission from the Philosophical Society. There are also Yakama songs (thirty minutes) by Leroy B. Selam of Monmouth, Oregon, made in the Library of Congress Recording Laboratory on December 12, 1975 (see Neaman, this volume, "Song Traditions of the Yakama").

The largest groups of noncylinder recordings from Washington State in the Archive of Folk Culture are the discs assembled by Willard Rhodes in 1947 and 1950. In 1938, Willard W. Beatty, director of Indian education for the Bureau of Indian Affairs, proposed a project that was to enlist the services of Rhodes, a professor of music at Columbia University. The two wanted to continue the tradition of documenting Native music begun by people such as Densmore, this time using improved disc—and, later, tape—technology that would be more readily accessible to the public. They also had the specific research goal of documenting the new kinds of music that were appearing side by side with traditional genres in Native communities.

Rhodes made nine field surveys between 1940 and 1952, including one brief visit to Washington at the end of July 1947 and a longer trip in August and September 1950. On the first trip he recorded three people on nine 12-inch discs at Toppenish; on the second he recorded at least twenty-seven people on eighteen reels of tape (approximately nine hours) in the communities of Auburn, Everson, La Conner, La Push, Marblemount, Marietta, Neah Bay, Shelton, and Union (see accompanying list). As in cases mentioned earlier, Rhodes's recordings and several notebooks containing field notes are in the Library of Congress, but much of the extant documentation is elsewhere. A substantial portion of Rhodes's papers and recordings were transmitted to the UCLA Ethnomusicology Archive in Los Angeles around 1983. In all, he gathered 260 disc recordings and fifty tapes, from which he was to select songs for a series of ten LPs to be made available to Indian schools and agencies, as well as to the general public through the Library of Congress.

Both Rhodes and Densmore were engaged in this process of providing increased access to their collections by means of publicly available sampler discs. In 1952, the Library released AFS L32, "Songs of the Nootka and Quileute," from the Densmore collection. Included were over thirty songs by nine singers. The jacket caption indicated that this record was "issued by the Library of Congress under a special grant for the preservation of Indian music." I have not found any production files or letters indicating that Densmore ever tried to get back to the singers to consult about the use of their songs in this way; by this time, of course, the recordings were twenty-five to thirty years old, and many of the singers were gone. But Densmore was clearly motivated by a sense that the recordings were important within Indian contexts and *should* be more important to the larger American society. In a letter dated April 30, 1946, for example, she wrote that "there is a definite future for Indian music and a need for its appreciation on the part of musicians. To the Indian, music was in the sphere of our oratorios and symphonies. The future will decide whether we, as a musical nation, rise to that appreciation of it." Or again, "[I]t looks as if Indian music needed a friend! I shall continue to do everything in my power to secure recognition of its poetic, if not its audible, interest but I think someone else ought to do more" (Densmore to Harold Spivacke, chief of the Library's Music Division, July 15, 1947). To that end, she wanted to see the recordings not only preserved but actively disseminated, particularly to composers and educators.

The Rhodes sampler discs, compiled within a few years of the time the recordings were originally collected, were handled differently with regard to permissions than the Densmore discs. In October 1951, Duncan Emrich, then chief of the Library's "Folklore Section," informed Rhodes that "sufficient funds have been transferred to the Recording Laboratory of the Library of Congress by the Bureau of Indian Affairs to permit our issuing one long-playing record from the Northwestern material collected by you." He asked Rhodes to select about nineteen minutes of material for each side. Rhodes chose a Skagit guardian spirit song, a Lummi paddling song, a story, several Chinook Jargon songs, several Shaker songs, a Klallam and a Quinault love song, a Quinault lullaby, two Tsaiyak Society songs, and four Makah bone game songs.

Rhodes then sought permission from the singers to use these specific songs. In March 1952 he began contacting Hannah Bowechop and Lyda Hottowe (Neah Bay), Tommie Bob (La Conner), Joseph Hillaire (Marietta), and Henry Allen (Union). Rhodes later noted that two additional singers, George Hottowe and Nellie Wilkie, were the son and daughter of Lyda Hottowe and were "covered in her voucher" (Rhodes letter of February 11, 1954, in Archive of Folk Culture production files for record album AFS L34). In return for a fee, each singer signed a contract granting the "Recording Laboratory of the Music Division of the Library of Congress permission to make and sell copies [of the listed songs] by pressing or to duplicate by any other process without further payment." The singers were paid by the minute, receiving amounts between $8 (1 minute, 34 seconds) and $65 (15 minutes, 47 seconds). It is difficult to pinpoint what these figures might mean in contemporary terms. According to the estimate in one statistical handbook, the purchasing power of a dollar in 1954 would have been the equivalent of $3.70 in 1982 dollars (and even more today), though there might have been considerable geographical variation. At the very least, the singers received the equivalent of $30 to $250 for their contributions.

The Rhodes sampler recordings were released in September 1954. The Northwest Coast album—AFS L34, "Northwest (Puget Sound)"—was accompanied by a booklet with rather extensive notes on each song, as well as an overview of Native cultures of western Washington written by Erna Gunther. Also included were quotations from Captain Cook and James Swan, who had observed musical practices in the area in 1778 and 1869, respectively.

The only other known ethnographic recordings from Washington State that are in Washington, D.C., are the discs in the John Peabody Harrington collection at the National Anthropological Archives in the Smithsonian Institution. These recordings were actually gathered by John Paul Marr, Harrington's field assistant, between April and June 1941. They include sixty-six discs containing Alsea vocabularies and stories recorded by John Albert of Oakville, Washington; thirty-six discs of Lower Chehalis stories recounted by Emma Luscier of Bay Center; sixteen discs of Chinook texts by Emma Luscier and Joe Peter, the latter from the Yakama reservation; thirty discs of Duwamish texts recorded by Peter James; seven discs of Lummi stories and dance songs from Patrick George of Bellingham; and four discs of stories and songs in what a computer printout lists as "Squalis lingo" (possibly a misreading of handwritten captions) recorded by George and Andrew Sandos. The documentation for these recordings is available on microfilm (see Mills 1981).

How do people outside of Washington, D.C., obtain access to the actual recordings of Washington State Native people's songs? What control do local communities have over the distribution of such materials? First, there are the published Densmore and Rhodes sampler recordings, which are still available through the Library of Congress. These recordings, sold at cost, are not eligible for copyright, since they were produced with tax dollars and thus belong to all of the people of the United States. This does not mean, however, that the recordings are in the public domain; proprietary rights remain with the performers or the performers' estates (generally the direct descendants). It is recommended that people interested in using or publishing the songs contact performers or their heirs for information and for permission.

The recommendations for the Archive of Folk Culture field recordings that were not published on sampler disks are shaped by similar considerations. As a federal agency, the Library of Congress must grant equal access to whose wishing to use materials in its collections. Unless materials came into the institution with specific restrictions or containing recordings made by commercial artists, the Library honors the request of anyone who wishes to order copies of collections for a personal project. This does not trigger a permissions search. However, if someone wants to order copies of material deposited in the Library with the intention of publishing—that is, replicating—those materials, he or she must first make a good-faith attempt to contact the performer or the performer's estate. The duplication process takes time and is expensive (currently $74 per hour). But it is an option open to anyone.

Library staff as well as researchers aware of Archive of Folk Culture collections have been concerned about the particular needs of the communities in which the recordings were originally made. People cannot always travel to Washington, D.C., to hear the recordings, and the cost of obtaining copies can be prohibitive (although in the past few years more federal and private grants that enable such purchases have become available for Indian communities seeking to reassemble information on their cultural heritage). For these reasons, the Library's American Folklife Center (the administrative unit encompassing the Archive of Folk Culture collections) undertook the Federal Cylinder Project. Created in 1979 to preserve, catalog, and disseminate copies of the early field recordings, the Cylinder Project contacted more than a hundred Indian communities, offering them free cassette copies of cylinder materials in the Archive of Folk Culture. See Schupman (1988), Gray (1990, 1991), and Lee (1992); the articles by Gray (1991) and Lee, in particular, describe tensions inherent in the collections themselves, the institutional realities that govern dissemination efforts, and consequent reception and use of cylinder recordings. If asked to do so, staff members also consulted with these communities, offering technical assistance on archival projects, bibliographical references, and information on parallel projects and potential funding resources.

This has been an instance in which one small branch of a federal agency has essentially sidestepped some of the usual procedures in order to try to reestablish local access. There are limits to what is possible, however. The Cylinder Project's initial contacts had to be with the federally recognized tribal governments, rather than, for example, with individual families. The Project could make free copies only for the communities of origin; it did not have resources to make them for all interested or even related communities. For the same reason, the Folklife Center cannot make free replacement copies if sets of tapes are lost. Also, the Cylinder Project covered only those materials originally recorded on wax cylinders, not songs on wire, disc, or tape.

But the underlying hope and goal have been that the songs on cylinder would find their way to their appropriate homes.

In the case of the Washington-based collections, the Folklife Center contracted with Carey Caldwell (who previously had worked at the Suquamish Museum and is now a curator at the Oakland Museum) to carry out dissemination visits. On May 23, 1986, she returned a copy of the Densmore and Frachtenberg recordings to the Quileute community on the occasion of the annual Elders Week dinner and assembly. The tapes were placed in care of the Tribal School Enrichment Program, the staff of which intended to make copies, arranged by performer, for use by tribal members (Terri Tavenner, letter to Federal Cylinder Project, July 8, 1986).

Caldwell visited Neah Bay two months later, spending time with staff of the Makah Cultural and Research Center, people involved in the language program, and various elders. As has happened elsewhere, the consultation there revealed some questions about the reliability of Densmore's identifications; there were also concerns about performers' rights to sing certain songs. Vivian Lawrence, a member of the tribal council, accepted the cassette copies on behalf of the community, commenting that "our songs are our history." When Caldwell left, museum staff were in the process of drafting policies for the use of cylinder materials and permission for access that would be taken to the Tribal Council for approval. Helma Swan (a Makah tribal elder and author) and Dr. Ann Renker have since indicated that the Goose Dance was revived for the Makah Day celebration as a direct result of elders hearing the cylinder recordings (Swan and Renker, personal communication, 1992).

In the past, songs and narratives were recorded in disparate Indian communities, and the information—or part of it—was funneled to Washington, D.C. A sense of urgency impelled turn-of-the-century collectors; they thought Indian cultures were dying and, in the face of that possibility, hoped to document all facets of tribal lifeways and expression. The linguist J. P. Harrington, mentioned above, perhaps said it best in a poem he dedicated to fellow anthropologist C. Hart Merriam in 1922. The value Harrington placed on Native traditions is clear:

> Give not, give not the yawning graves their plunder;
>> Save, save the lore, for future ages' joy:
> The stories full of beauty and of wonder,
>> The songs more pristine than the songs of Troy,
> The ancient speech, forever to be vanished—

> Lore that tomorrow to the grave goes down!
> All other thought from our horizon banished,
> Let any sacrifice our labor crown.
> (cited in Walsh 1976:15)

In looking back, we may indeed question some of the presumptions behind the collecting ventures, as well as the tactics used by various collectors. And yet Harrington's vision has, to a certain extent, come true. The net effect of the documentary efforts of people like Densmore, Frachtenberg, Harrington, Rhodes, and Swadesh is that some material that might have been lost was not; continuity of some songs and change in others are demonstrated by recordings nearly a century old. Some traditions were indeed "saved," albeit outside of the community, for "future ages' joy"—that is, for present and future generations engaged in documenting their own cultural traditions. What was once an activity undertaken by outsiders on short visits is now more often the lifework of members of the communities. And everyone has been made aware that cultural expressions such as songs are significant and deserving of respect.

Times have changed. Where once the impulse was to gather everything and bring it back to Washington, D.C., there are signs of willingness and desire in most federal agencies to facilitate access, to return information, to encourage and assist community documentation and archival preservation of these efforts. Dissemination is an idea whose time has clearly come, though there are limits to what federal agencies can or should do. But, bit by bit—even though issues of community access to, and control of, the materials are not always easily resolved—the process of cultural preservation in Indian communities goes on.

Notes

1. For example, Paul Radin, who worked with Winnebago consultants between 1908 and 1913, recorded some of their songs on cylinders but in his major ethnography added this disclaimer: "Certain subjects, such as mythology, art, and music, have been entirely omitted. In order to discuss . . . [music], specific training and knowledge were demanded, which the author does not possess" (Radin 1923:47).

2. Densmore identified Makah Day as "an annual celebration in commemoration of the visit of the Wanamaker Expedition . . . characterized by the giving of old, important dances by expert dancers. . . . The purpose of the dancing was to instruct the younger people in the traditions and old customs of the tribe" (Densmore 1939:128).

3. In listing the songs by tribal source, Densmore made a cataloging decision that is different from the one we at the Library of Congress now generally make. We list each song ac-

cording to the tribal affiliation of the singer, operating on the principle that if members of one community can sing a "foreign" song, it means that the song has in some sense been incorporated into local repertory and may no longer sound exactly as it would if sung by a member of the "foreign" society in which the song originated. For example, in the Federal Cylinder Project catalogs, Young Doctor's "song of the guests in their canoes," which Densmore lists as "Quinault," is included among the Makah entries.

JUDITH GRAY, head of reference in the American Folklife Center at the Library of Congress, has been with the Federal Cylinder Project since 1983. Trained as an ethnomusicologist at Wesleyan University, she is part of the team that assembled *Many Nations: A Library of Congress Resource Guide for the Study of Indian and Alaskan Native Peoples of the United States* (Library of Congress, 1996).

People who performed for Willard Rhodes

Performer	Date	Location	Types of Songs Identified
Oscar Beavert and his mother, Mrs. Alex Saluskin	1947	Toppenish	
Charley Jim			
George Young	1950	Auburn	Puyallup, Nisqually, Lummi, and "Canadian"
Mr. and Mrs. William Gus			Snohomish
Betsy Lozier			Snoqualmie
Charles Anderson	1950	Everson	Nooksack, Skagit
Mr. and Mrs. Tommy Bob	1950	La Conner	Samish, Swinomish, and Shaker
Stanley Gray	1950	La Push	Quileute, Chinook
Mr. and Mrs. Harry Moses	1950	Marblemount	Shaker
Mrs. Jessie Moses			Shaker
Joseph Hillaire	1950	Marietta	Samyama, Lummi, etc.
Helen Peterson	1950	Neah Bay	Nitinat
Lyda Hottowe			Makah, Shaker
George Hottowe			Klallam, Makah
Maggie Alderson			Clayoquot
Mr. and Mrs. Charles Swan			Makah, Kwakiutl
Hannah Bowechop			Quinault, Shaker
Nellie Wilkie			Klallam, Makah
Patrick Wilkie			
Family of Charley Jones			
Randolph Parker			
Alec Green			
John Hawk, Jerry Meeker	1950	Shelton	Skokomish, Puyallup
Henry Allen	1950	Union	Klallam, Puyallup, Chehalis, Chinook, Twana, Nisqually

Appendix 3

Melville Jacobs and Early Ethnographic
Recordings in the Northwest

WILLIAM R. SEABURG

MELVILLE JACOBS (1902–71) WAS A PROMINENT NORTHWEST
anthropologist, noted for his studies of Native languages and oral traditions. Less
well-known is the fact that Jacobs was a major collector of Northwest Native musical
traditions as well, collecting and documenting more recordings than perhaps any
other fieldworker in Oregon and Washington.

Jacobs was a professor in the Department of Anthropology at the University of
Washington from 1928 to 1971. His primary research focus was the Indian languages
and cultures of the Pacific Northwest, especially those of western Oregon and eastern
Washington.

From 1926 to 1939, Jacobs spent up to six months of each year collecting Native
American linguistic, folkloric, and ethnographic materials, often by means of pho-
netically recorded texts with translations. He also made audio recordings, at first using the small Edison phonograph wax cylinders (recording time 3–4 minutes), then
the larger Ediphone wax cylinders (recording time 8–9 minutes), and finally RCA
Victor pre-grooved phonograph records, made on a portable electric phonograph he
had built especially for his research (recording time 5–6 minutes total for the two
sides). Jacobs was sometimes assisted in the field by his wife, Elizabeth D. Jacobs,
who wrote the documentation to accompany their Tillamook and Upper Coquille
Athabaskan records.

In December 1933, Jacobs received a grant of $242.50 from the National Research Council's Grants-in-Aid program for the construction of a portable electric phonograph recorder. The machine, constructed by "Mr. Philip A. Jacobsen (of the department of General Engineering of the University of Washington) and his assistant Mr. Orin Johnston," was "first put to use with Mrs. [Annie Miner] Peterson on Coos Bay," Oregon, in July 1934 (Jacobs 1939:5). The recording equipment is now located in the Burke Museum of Natural History and Culture, University of Washington, Seattle.

All told, Jacobs recorded 105 wax cylinders and 80 acetate and aluminum discs, representing approximately 524 songs. The songs are tokens of many different song types, including spirit power songs, war songs, shaman's songs, gambling songs, lullabies, love charm songs, songs from myth texts, root-digging and berry-picking songs, fun songs, children's game songs, and Ghost Dance songs (Seaburg 1982). Jacobs recorded not only the music but also ethnographic notes about the songs, including transcriptions and translations of any words or vocables, the name of the person from whom the singer had learned the song, the type of song it was, and the like. Especially noteworthy are the extensive notes accompanying the Clackamas Chinook recordings of 1929 and 1930 from Victoria Howard.

The primary purpose of the wax cylinder recordings was to preserve the music. The recording time was too short to record most folklore or ethnographic texts without continually interrupting the performance in order to change the record; besides, such texts could be satisfactorily transcribed by hand in notebooks. Music, on the other hand, presented a problem: Jacobs felt that it was "impossible to describe non-European music through field recording techniques utilizing pencil and paper. In the field-work situation the musicologist cannot write fast enough, or make note of every feature of musical style. Moreover, his ear must become attuned to subtle features of intonation and rhythm which are new to his experience. He begins to perceive these only after prolonged familiarity and repeated careful listening" (Jacobs and Stern 1955:237–38).

According to Jacobs, the "major scientific function" of the acetate and the longer-playing aluminum phonograph records, besides providing better fidelity, was to "permit checking and corroboration by other scientists of the analysis made on paper by the linguist who went into the field." Jacobs emphasized that the records' main function in this regard was not for *primary* documentation of linguistic material, "but as a later means of rechecking of the slips, notebooks, and later printed data" (Jacobs ca. 1945:769). In fact, Jacobs did not make many records of word lists or of connected speech (folklore or ethnographic texts). The bulk of his audio recordings—both cylinders and discs—is of Native music.

Although Jacobs had early musical training—he studied violin at the Institute of Musical Art (Juilliard Conservatory) from 1917 to 1920 (Thompson 1978:640)—he was not trained as an ethnomusicologist and did not consider himself to be one. Why, then, did he make so many recordings of Indian music? The answer lies in part in his graduate training at Columbia University with Franz Boas, who urged the documentation of *all* aspects of expressive culture, including music. Boas himself made wax cylinder recordings of Kwakw̲aka'wakw (Kwakiutl) music at least as early as 1893 at the World's Columbian Exposition in Chicago (Lee 1984:30).

A second factor was the dearth of trained ethnomusicologists willing and able to do the work. Jacobs felt that there was not time to wait for an ethnomusicologist to arrive on the scene, because the musical traditions were fast disappearing. Indeed, he was right. In a letter written in ca. 1929 or 1930 to George Herzog (Archives of Traditional Music [ATM], Indiana University, Bloomington), Jacobs reported, "The last few weeks I recorded a few score Clackamas, Molale and Twalatin songs by one lady in northwest Oregon—a perfect gold mine of material from three virtually extinct tribes; every day she sings more." That "lady in northwest Oregon" was Victoria Howard, one of the last speakers of the Clackamas Chinook language, who died later in 1930. The only known sound recordings of Clackamas Chinook music are those Jacobs made with Mrs. Howard.

Yet another major impetus to Jacobs's music collecting probably came from his friendship with the ethnomusicologist George Herzog (1901–83). Herzog and Jacobs were fellow graduate students at Columbia in the mid-1920s under Franz Boas's direction. Although the American Museum of Natural History supplied the wax cylinders for Jacobs's first audio recordings, during the summer of 1927 they were recorded on a "small German machine" that Herzog had loaned Jacobs (letter from Jacobs to Herzog, December 7, 1941, Melville Jacobs Collection [MJC], University of Washington Libraries, Seattle). There is evidence in Jacobs's correspondence (and elsewhere) that Jacobs had Herzog in mind when he made his music recordings. In a letter to Herzog (ca. 1929 or 1930, ATM), Jacobs wrote: "I hope to get some Santiam Kalapuya songs this summer also. Then, with Chehalis-Cowlitz (now in N.Y.), Klikitat, Twalatin, Molale, Clackamas and Kalapuya you will be able to do a coherent job, when you wish, on the region. . . ." In a letter to Boas regarding Jacobs's fieldwork with Miluk and Hanis Coos (October 11, 1933, MJC), Jacobs noted, "I also secured sixty odd songs which should give Herzog a sampling of coastal Oregon music."

While Jacobs made the occasional music notation in his field notebooks, he did not transcribe or analyze any of the musical compositions he so carefully recorded. He did attempt—for the most part unsuccessfully—to interest ethnomusicologists in the task. Originally Herzog was slated to "work up" the music recordings. In a letter to Robert H. Lowie (May 17, 1932, MJC), Jacobs wrote, "I think it wiser to have Herzog do the work than his friend Kolinsky in Berlin, because the Adamson-Gunther-Jacobs Northwest records at the Museum of Natural History in New York are to be done by Herzog, and it is better that he handle the entire collection consistently." E. M. von Hornbostel (letters from Jacobs to Herzog, July 10 and August 10, 1932, ATM) had urged Jacobs to employ Mieczyslaw Kolinski to transcribe Jacobs's Victoria Howard recordings, but Jacobs did not have the approximately $700 needed to employ Kolinski for a year to transcribe the twenty-seven Ediphone cylinders.

Eventually Herzog did transcribe the 1929–30 Victoria Howard Clackamas Chinook recordings (Seeger and Spear 1987:75), and one of the songs from this collection was published in "Special Song Types in North American Indian Music" (Herzog 1935). However, none of the rest of Jacobs's music recordings are known to have been transcribed, analyzed, or published (see Graf 1986).

In 1941, the composer-folklorist Béla Bartók (1881–1945) was expected to come to the University of Washington, and he agreed to work with Jacobs's music recordings (letter from Jacobs to Herzog, December 7, 1941, MJC). Unfortunately, ill health prevented Bartók from joining the University's music faculty, and the potentially fruitful collaboration did not materialize.

The purpose of the music recordings was to preserve what Jacobs perceived to be a fast-disappearing aspect of Native American expressive culture before it was too late. Preservation, however, was not considered an end in itself. Jacobs was not nostalgic about the loss of Native languages and cultures, nor was he interested in Native cultural renaissance. The recordings were for the advancement of the nascent science of ethnomusicology and were to remain unplayed until such time as reliable copies could be made or a competent musicologist could work with them. Above all else, Jacobs believed in science. When a descendant of one of his consultants wrote to him asking for a copy of the recordings he had obtained from her mother, Jacobs wrote back that, because the delicate wax cylinders needed to be preserved for their scientific study, he could not oblige her.

Jacobs also took a dim view of amateur collectors. In response to a letter of inquiry from the author, then an undergraduate at Western Washington State College, regarding fieldwork on the nearby Nooksack language, Jacobs added in a postscript: "Does Dr. Bowman have either training or experience in linguistic research in tough field situations? After all, we don't encourage amateurs to do research in cyclotron buildings, or in chem labs. Forgive the snarl; but I am quite concerned about amateurism" (Jacobs, June 4, 1969; Elizabeth Bowman was Seaburg's linguistic professor at WWSC). Jacobs was afraid such amateurs might alienate the Native people and spoil things for later, more "scientific" anthropological or linguistic fieldworkers. Besides, it was not enough simply to collect samples of music. One needed to document the songs fully with reliable linguistic transcriptions and relevant ethnographic annotation. Jacobs discouraged "amateur" collectors of Northwest Indian language and music such as Leon Metcalf. Fortunately for us, Metcalf made his recordings anyway, and they have proven a valuable resource for both research and cultural revival. (Lushootseed elder and scholar Vi [taqʷšəblu] Hilbert has made extensive use of Metcalf's tape recordings of several Lushootseed speakers from the 1950s. The Metcalf recordings are in the Anthropology Archives, Burke Museum of Natural History and Culture, University of Washington, Seattle.)

Jacobs was important not only for the Native American sound recordings he himself made; he also maintained for safekeeping original and duplicate copies of the sound recordings of students and colleagues, including Vivian Williams, Arthur C. Ballard, Viola Garfield, William W. Elmendorf, and others (Seaburg 1982:112). As a major collector of Northwest Native American music and a rigorous scholar, he has had a lasting influence on the collection and study of the First People's musical traditions. The information he gathered—including not only the songs themselves but sometimes extensive documentation of their provenance, use, and significance—remains a valuable resource for both ethnomusicologists and Native peoples seeking knowledge of traditional ways.

WILLIAM R. SEABURG received his Ph.D. in anthropology from the University of Washington in 1994. His research interests include Native American expressive culture and the history of anthropological fieldwork among Native Americans in the Pacific Northwest.

Bibliography

Adamson, Thelma. 1934. *Folk-Tales of the Coast Salish*. Memoirs of the American Folklore Society 27. New York: G. E. Stechert.

Amoss, Pamela. 1972. "The Persistence of Aboriginal Beliefs and Practices Among the Nooksack Coast Salish." Ph.D. diss., University of Washington.

————. 1978a. *Coast Salish Spirit Dancing: The Survival of an Ancestral Religion*. Seattle: University of Washington Press.

————. 1978b. "Symbolic Substitution in the Indian Shaker Church." *Ethnohistory* 25(3): 225–49.

————. 1982. "Resurrection, Healing, and 'the Shake': The Story of John and Mary Slocum." In *Charisma and Sacred Biography*, ed. Michael A. Williams. *Journal of the American Academy of Religion*, Thematic Studies 48(3–4): 87–109.

————. 1988. "Erna Gunther." In *Women Anthropologists: A Biographical Dictionary*, ed. Ute Gacs et al., pp. 133–39. New York: Greenwood Press.

————. 1990. "The Indian Shaker Church." In *Handbook of North American Indians (Northwest Coast)*, ed. Wayne Suttles, 7:633–39. Washington, D.C.: Smithsonian Institution.

Ballard, Arthur. 1929. *Mythology of Southern Puget Sound*. University of Washington Publications in Anthropology 3(2): 31–150. Seattle: University of Washington Press.

Barnett, H. G. 1957. *Indian Shakers: A Messianic Cult of the Pacific Northwest*. Carbondale: Southern Illinois University Press.

Boas, Franz. 1888. "Chinook Songs." *Journal of American Folklore* 1(3): 220–26.

———. 1972. The Professional Correspondence of Franz Boas [microfilm]. Wilmington, Del.: Scholarly Resources.

Bradley, Ian L. 1976. "Indian Music of the Pacific Northwest: An Annotated Bibliography of Research." *B.C. Studies* 31(Autumn): 12–22.

Buchanan, Charles Milton (Agent). 1914. "The So-Called 'Shaker Indians of the Northwest.'" *Annual Report: Tulalip Reservation, Washington.*

Castile, George P. 1982. "The 'Half Catholic' Movement: Edwin and Myron Eells and the Rise of the Indian Shaker Church." *Pacific Northwest Quarterly* 73(4): 165–74.

Colson, Elizabeth. 1953. *The Makah Indians.* Minneapolis: University of Minnesota Press.

Commissioner of Indian Affairs. 1890. *Annual Report of the Commissioner of Indian Affairs to the Secretary of the Interior.*

Curtis, Edward S. 1916. *The North American Indian.* Volume 11. Norwood, Mass.: Plimpton Press.

Densmore, Frances. n.d. Diaries and diary summaries. MS. 4250, National Anthropological Archives. Washington, D.C.: Smithsonian Institution.

———. [1911] 1970. *The North American Indians.* Volumes 7, 8, 9, 10, 11, 18, 20. New York: Johnson Reprint.

———. [1939] 1972. *Nootka and Quileute Music.* Smithsonian Institution, Bureau of American Ethnology, Bulletin 124. Reprint. New York: Da Capo Press.

———. 1940. Report on recording equipment used in recording Indian songs for the Bureau of American Ethnology. Typescript dated March 27. (Photocopy, Archive of Folk Culture files.)

———. 1941. "The Study of Indian Music." *Annual Report of the Board of Regents of the Smithsonian Institution Showing the Operations, Expenditures, and Condition of the Institution for the Year Ended June 30, 1941*, pp. 527–50. Washington, D.C.

———. 1943. *Music of the Indians of British Columbia.* Bureau of American Ethnology, Bulletin 136.

Drucker, Philip. 1951. *The Northern and Central Nootkan Tribes.* Bureau of American Ethnology, Bulletin 144.

DuBois, Cora. 1938. *The Feather Cult of the Middle Columbia.* General Series in Anthropology 7. Menasha, Wisc.: Banta.

Eells, Myron. 1879. "Indian Music." *American Antiquarian* 1(4): 249–53.

———. 1892. "Shaking Religion." *American Missionary* 46(5): 157–58. New York.

———. 1985. *The Indians of Puget Sound: The Notebooks of Myron Eells*, ed. George P. Castile. Seattle: University of Washington Press.

Ellingson, Ter. 1992. "Transcription." In *Ethnomusicology: An Introduction*, ed. Helen Myers, pp. 110–52. New York: W. W. Norton.

Elmendorf, William W. 1960. *The Structure of Twana Culture.* Washington State University Research Studies, Monographic Supplement 2.

Ernst, Alice. 1952. *The Wolf Ritual of the Northwest Coast.* Eugene: University of Oregon Press.

Fitzpatrick, Darleen Ann. 1968. "The 'Shake': The Indian Shaker Curing Ritual Among the Yakima." Master's thesis, University of Washington.

Frisbie, Charlotte J. 1991. "Women and the Society for Ethnomusicology: Roles and Contributions from Formation Through Incorporation (1952/53–1961)." In *Comparative Musicology and Anthropology of Music: Essays on the History of Ethnomusicology,* ed. Bruno Nettl and Philip V. Bohlman, pp. 244–65. Chicago: University of Chicago Press.

Galpin, F. W. 1903. "The Whistles and Reed Instruments of the American Indians of the Northwest Coast." *Royal Musical Association, Proceedings* 29:115–38.

Goodman, Linda J. 1974. Field Notes, Tapes, Transcripts of Interviews with Helma Swan Ward (1974–94).

———. 1977. *Music and Dance in Northwest Coast Indian Life.* Occasional Papers, vol. 3, Music and Dance Series 3. Tsaile, Arizona: Navajo Community College Press.

———. 1978. "This is *My* Song: The Role of Song as Symbol in Makah Life." Ph.D. diss., Washington State University.

———. 1986. "Nootka Music." *The New Grove Dictionary of American Music* 3:330–82. London: Macmillan Press, Ltd.

———. 1991. "Traditional Music in Makah Life." In *A Time of Gathering: Native Heritage in Washington State,* ed. Robin K. Wright, pp. 223–33. Seattle: University of Washington Press.

———. 1992. "Aspects of Spiritual and Political Power in Chiefs' Songs of the Makah Indians." *The World of Music, Journal of the International Institute for Traditional Music* 34(2): 23–42.

Gould, Richard A., and Theodore P. Furukawa. 1964. "Aspects of Ceremonial Life Among the Indian Shakers of Smith River, California." *Kroeber Anthropological Society Papers* 35:51–67.

Graf, Marilyn. 1986. "The Papers of George Herzog." *Resound: A Quarterly of the Archives of Traditional Music* 5(1).

Gray, Judith A., ed. 1988. *The Federal Cylinder Project: A Guide to Field Cylinder Collections in Federal Agencies.* Volume 3: *Great Basin/Plateau Indian Catalog; Northwest Coast/ Arctic Indian Catalog.* Washington, D.C.: American Folklife Center.

———. 1990. "Documenting Native America with Sound Recordings: The First 100 Years of Federal Involvement." *Folklife Center News* 12(1): 4–7.

———. 1991. "The Songs Come Home—The Federal Cylinder Project." *CRM* 14(5): 32–35.

Gunther, Erna. n.d. "Analysis of the First Salmon Ceremony." *American Anthropologist* 28: 605–17.

———. 1925. *Klallam Folk Tales*. University of Washington Publications in Anthropology 1(4): 113–70. Seattle: University of Washington Press.

———. 1927. *Klallam Ethnography*. University of Washington Publications in Anthropology 1(5): 171–314. Seattle: University of Washington Press.

———. 1949. "The Shaker Religion of the Northwest." In *Indians of the Urban Northwest*, ed. Marian W. Smith, pp. 36–77. New York: Columbia University Press.

Haeberlin, Hermann. 1924. "Mythology of Puget Sound." *Journal of American Folklore* 37(145–46): 371–438.

———, and Erna Gunther. 1930. *The Indians of Puget Sound*. University of Washington Publications in Anthropology 4(1): 1–84. Seattle: University of Washington Press.

Handbook of North American Indians. 1990. Volume 7, *Northwest Coast*; Volume 12, *Plateau* (in progress). Washington, D.C.: Smithsonian Institution.

Harmon, Ray. 1965. "Indian Shaker Church of The Dalles, Oregon, 1896–1920." *Oregon Historical Quarterly* 72 (June 1971): 148–58.

Herzog, George. 1935. "Special Song Types in North American Indian Music." *Zeitschrift für vergleichende Musikwissenschaft* 3(1/2): 23–33.

———. 1949. "Salish Music." In *Indians of the Urban Northwest*, ed. Marian W. Smith, pp. 93–109. New York: Columbia University Press.

Jacobs, Melville. 1939. *Coos Narrative and Ethnologic Texts*. University of Washington Publications in Anthropology 8(1): 1–126. Seattle: University of Washington Press.

———. "Handbook for Field Recording of Primitive Languages" [ca. 1945]. Melville Jacobs Collection, University of Washington Libraries, Seattle.

———, and Bernhard J. Stern. 1955. *General Anthropology*, 2d ed. New York: Barnes and Noble.

Jones, Judith Ann. 1995. "'Women Never Used to War Dance': Gender and Music in Nez Perce Culture Change." Ph.D. diss., Washington State University.

Josephy, Alvin M., Jr. 1965. *The Nez Perce Indians and the Opening of the Northwest*. New Haven and London: Yale University Press.

Judd, Neil. 1967. *The Bureau of American Ethnology: A Partial History*. Norman: University of Oklahoma Press.

Lee, Dorothy Sara, ed. 1984. *The Federal Cylinder Project: A Guide to Field Cylinder Collections in Federal Agencies*. Volume 8: *Early Anthologies*. Washington, D.C.: American Folklife Center.

———. 1992. "Historic Recordings and Contemporary Native American Culture: Returning Materials to Native American Communities." In *Music and Dance of Aboriginal Australia and the South Pacific: The Effects of Documentation on the Living Tradition,* ed. Alice M. Moyle, pp. 24–39. Sydney: University of Sydney Press.

Merriam, Alan P. 1967. *Ethnomusicology of the Flathead Indians.* Chicago: Aldine.

Mills, Elaine L., ed. 1981. *The Papers of John Peabody Harrington in the Smithsonian Institution, 1907–1957.* Volume 1: *A Guide to the Field Notes: Native American History, Language, and Culture of Alaska/Northwest Coast.* White Plains, N.Y.: Kraus International Publications.

Mohling, Virginia Gill. 1957. "Twana Spirit Power Songs." Master's thesis, University of Washington.

Mooney, James. 1896. "The Ghost-Dance Religion and the Sioux Outbreak of 1890." *14th Annual Report of the Bureau of American Ethnology for the Years 1892–1893.* Part 2. Washington, D.C.

Nettl, Bruno. 1954. *North American Indian Musical Styles.* Philadelphia: American Folklore Society.

Olsen, Loran. 1979. "The Nez Perce Flute." *Northwest Anthropological Research Notes* 13(1): 36–44.

———. 1989. *Guide to the Nez Perce Music Archive: An Annotated Listing of Songs and Musical Selections Spanning the Period 1897–1974.* Pullman: Washington State University Press.

Peck, Elizabeth Tuckwiller. 1973. "Songs of the Bogachiel: An Examination of the Music Owned by a Prestigious Quileute Family." Master's thesis, Washington State University.

Peterson, Jacqueline. 1993. *Sacred Encounters: Father DeSmet and the Indians of the Rocky Mountain West.* Norman and London: Washington State University and University of Oklahoma Press.

Radin, Paul. 1923. "The Winnebago Tribe." *Thirty-seventh Annual Report of the Bureau of American Ethnology, 1915–1916.* Washington, D.C.: Government Printing Office.

Reagan, Albert B. 1908. "The Shake Dance of the Quileute Indians, with Drawing by an Indian Pupil of the Quileute Day School." In *Proceedings of the Indiana Academy of Science, 1908,* pp. 71–74. Indianapolis.

———. 1910. "Notes on the Shaker Church of the Indians." In *Proceedings of the Indiana Academy of Science, 1910,* pp. 115–16. Indianapolis.

Rhodes, Willard. 1954. "Shaker Church Songs." *Music of the American Indian: Northwest (Puget Sound).* Washington, D.C.: Library of Congress Recording AFS L34. Accompanying booklet, pp. 17–19.

———. 1974. "Music of the North American Indian Shaker Religion." *Studia Instrumen-*

torum Musicae Popularis III: Festschrift to Ernst Emsheimer on the Occasion of His 70th Birthday, January 15th 1974, ed. Gustaf Hilleström, pp. 180–84. Stockholm: Musikhistoriska Museet.

Richen, Marily C. 1974. "Legitimacy and the Resolution of Conflict in an Indian Church." Ph.D. diss., University of Oregon.

Roberts, Helen H. 1936. *Musical Areas in Aboriginal North America*. Yale University Publications in Anthropology 12. New Haven: Yale University Press.

————, and H. K. Haeberlin. 1918. "Some Songs of the Puget Sound Salish." *Journal of American Folklore* 31:496–520.

————, and Morris Swadesh. 1955. "Songs of the Nootka Indians of Western Vancouver Island." *Transactions of the American Philosophical Society* 45(3): 199–327.

Rohner, Ronald P., ed. 1969. *The Ethnography of Franz Boas: Letters and Diaries of Franz Boas Written on the Northwest Coast from 1886–1931*. Chicago: University of Chicago Press.

Sapir, Edward. 1911. "Some Aspects of Nootka Language and Culture." *American Anthropologist*, n.s. 13:15–28.

————. 1913. "A Girl's Puberty Ceremony Among the Nootka." *Transactions of the Royal Society of Canada*, 3d series, 7(2): 67–80.

————, and Morris Swadesh. 1939. "Nootka Texts." *Linguistic Society of America*. Philadelphia: University of Pennsylvania.

————. 1955. "Native Accounts of Nootka Ethnography." *International Journal of American Linguistics* 21(2): 1–452.

Schupman, Edwin J., Jr. 1988. "Northern Cheyennes Preserve Tribal Culture." *Folklife Center News* 10(2): 10–13.

Schuster, Helen Hersh. 1975. "Yakima Indian Traditionalism: A Study in Continuity and Change." Ph.D. diss., University of Washington.

Seaburg, William R. 1982. *Guide to Pacific Northwest Native American Materials in the Melville Jacobs Collection and in Other Archival Collections in the University of Washington Libraries*. Seattle: University of Washington Libraries.

Seeger, Anthony, and Louise S. Spear. 1987. *Early Field Recordings: A Catalogue of Cylinder Collections at the Indiana University Archives of Traditional Music*. Bloomington: Indiana University Press.

Smith, Marion W. 1940. *The Puyallup-Nisqually*. New York: Columbia University Press.

Smithsonian Institution. 1917. *Smithsonian Miscellaneous Collections* 66(17). Washington, D.C.: Government Printing Office.

Spier, Leslie. 1935. *The Prophet Dance of the Northwest and Its Derivatives: The Source of the Ghost Dance*. Menasha, Wisc.: Banta.

Sproat, Gilbert M. 1868. *Scenes and Studies of Savage Life*. London: Smith, Elder, and Co.

Stern, Bernhard J. 1934. *The Lummi Indians of Northwest Washington*. New York: Columbia University Press.

Stuart, Wendy Bross. 1972. *Gambling Music of the Coast Salish Indians*. Ottawa: National Museums of Canada, Ethnology Division.

Swan, James G. 1870. *The Indians of Cape Flattery*. Smithsonian Contributions to Knowledge 16. Smithsonian Institution Publication 220.

Teit, James. 1936. "The Salishan Tribes of the Western Plateau." *Annual Report, Bureau of American Ethnology* 45(1927–36): 23–396.

Thompson, Laurence C. 1978. "Melville Jacobs (1902–1971)." *American Anthropologist* 80: 640–46.

Valory, Dale. 1966. "The Focus of Indian Shaker Healing." *Kroeber Anthropological Society Papers* 35:67–112.

Walsh, Jane MacLaren. 1976. *John Peabody Harrington: The Man and His California Indian Fieldnotes*. Ramona, Calif.: Ballena Press.

Waterman, T. T. 1922. "The Shake Religion of Puget Sound." In *Annual Report of the Board of Regents of the Smithsonian Institution*, pp. 499–507. Washington, D.C.: Government Printing Office.

Wickwire, Wendy C. 1982. "Cultures in Contact: Music, the Plateau Indian, and the Western Encounter." Ph.D. diss., Wesleyan University, Middletown, Conn.

———. 1985. "Theories of Ethnomusicology and the North American Indian: Retrospective and Critique." *Canadian University Music Review* 6:186–221.

Williams, Melda. 1967. "Historical Background and Musical Analysis of Thirty Selected Nez Perce Songs." Master's thesis, University of Idaho.

Williams, Vivian Thomlinson. 1962. "Analysis of Skagit Music." Master's thesis, University of Washington.

Zimmerly, David D. 1974. *Museocinematography: Ethnographic Film Programs of the National Museum of Man, (1913–1973)*. Ottawa: National Museums of Canada, Ethnology Division.

Recommended Recordings

Creation's Journey: Native American Music, selected by Dr. Charlotte Heth (1992 and 1993). Smithsonian Folkways C-SF 40410.

Folk Music of the United States—Northwest (Puget Sound) (1947). Library of Congress AFS L34.

Heartbeat: Voices of the First Nation's Women. Wasco-Wishram (1995). Smithsonian Folkways.

Indian Music of the Pacific Northwest Coast, collected and recorded by Dr. Ida Halpern (1967). Folkways FE4523.

Intertribal Pow-wow Songs—Treaty of 1855. Yakima-Wasco (1980). Canyon CR-6173-C.

Music of the Nez Perce (1991); *Nez Perce Stories* (1991). Wild Sanctuary (124 9th Avenue, San Francisco, CA 94118). WSC 1602 and 1601.

Nootka Indian Music of the Pacific Northwest Coast, collected, recorded, and annotated by Dr. Ida Halpern (1974). Folkways FE4524.

Omak Pow-wow (1980). Canyon CR-6175-C.

Red Cedar: Winter Medicine Songs; Spring Medicine Songs; Summer Medicine Songs; Fire Circle Songs, by Johnny Moses (1979). Red Cedar Circle (P.O. Box 1210, La Conner, WA 98257).

Sam Morris Collection (Denoised): 60 Nez Perce, 1 Chinook Jargon (1995). Compact disc. WSU, ATM, AFC. NW Interpretive Association (909 1st Avenue, Suite 630, Seattle, WA 98104-1060).

Songs and Stories from Neah Bay, by Helen Peterson of the Makah Tribe (1976). Canyon C6125.

Songs of a Yakima Encampment (1975). Canyon CR-6129.

Songs of the Warm Springs Indian Reservation (1974). Canyon CR-6123.

Stick Game Songs, a live recording of a stick game in progress, Arlee Powwow, Montana (1972). Canyon CR-6174-C.

Ya-Ka-Ma Singers (1989). Meninick (P.O. Box 561, Toppenish, WA 98948).

Yakima Nation Singers of Satus Longhouse (1975). Canyon CR-6126-C.

Sacred Encounters (1993). Lawrence Johnson Productions (P.O. Box 14384, Portland, OR 97214).

Recommended Movies and Videos

Everything Change [Wenatchi]. Ellensburg Public Library, Ellensburg, WA 98926.

Ethnographic Film Programs, National Museums of Canada—*Bella Coola Dancers; Coast Salish Indians of British Columbia; Cultus Lake [Coast Salish]; Pole Raising [Kwakiutl]; Saving the Sagas; The Bella Coola Indians of British Columbia; The Kootenay Indians of British Columbia; The Nootka Indians of British Columbia; The Shuswap Indians of British Columbia; The Tsimshian Indians of the Skeena River of British Columbia*. Ethnology Division, National Museums of Canada, Ottawa.

In the Land of the War Canoes [Kwakiutl]. University of Washington, Burke Memorial Museum, Seattle, WA 98105.

Native Music of the Northwest Series (1981)—*Makah Songs by Helen Peterson Nee Mee Poo* [Nez Perce]; *Lummi Indian Music and Heritage*, with Joe Washington; *Sla-hal, the Bone Game* [Makah]; *Squaxin Island Wedding; Tulalip Coast Salish Pow-wow Club; Tulalip Salmon Ceremony*. Instructional Media Services, Washington State University, Pullman, WA 99164.

Potlatch: A Strict Law Bids Us Dance. Shandel and Wheeler. Media Exchange Cooperative, AV Centres, Post-Secondary Institutions in British Columbia.

Real People Series (1976)—*Awakening* [Flathead]; *Buffalo, Blood, Salmon and Roots* [Flathead, Kalispel]; *Circle of Song* [Coeur d'Alene]; *Legend of the Stick Game* [Kalispel, Coeur d'Alene]; *Mainstream* [Coeur d'Alene]; *Season of Grandmothers* [Spokane, Wenatchee, Flathead, Coeur d'Alene]; *Spirit of the Wind* [Okanogan, Omak, Flathead]; *Words of Life, People of Rivers* [Okanogan, Spokane, Colville]. Native American Public Broadcasting Consortium, Lincoln, NE 68504.

Further Resources

American Folklife Center   202-707-5510
Library of Congress   (reference inquiries)
Washington, D.C. 20540-8100

National Anthropological Archives   202-357-1986
National Museum of Natural History
Smithsonian Institution
Washington, D.C. 20560

American Philosophical Society Library 215-440-3400
105 South 5th Street
Philadelphia, PA 19106

Index

Numbers in **boldface** type refer to illustrations; those in *italic* refer to captions.